NUTS AND BOLTS OF DAILY SPIRITUALITY

NUTS & BOLTS
of Daily
Spirituality

PRACTICAL STEPS TO
draw closer TO GOD

DAVID M. KNIGHT

TWENTY
THIRD *23rd*
PUBLICATIONS
NEW LONDON, CT 06320
WWW.23RDPUBLICATIONS.COM

Twenty-Third Publications
A Division of Bayard
One Montauk Avenue, Suite 200
New London, CT 06320
(860) 437-3012 or (800) 321-0411
www.23rdpublications.com

ISBN: 978-1-58595-920-4
Library of Congress Catalog Card Number : 2013945643
Printed in the U.S.A.

TABLE OF CONTENTS

FOREWORD

This book is about the "nuts and bolts" of daily spirituality. You won't find a book that presents more simply and concretely what you have to do to grow to that *fullness of life* that is the *perfection of love*. This is a ground-level book.

At the same time, you will not find many books (in readable English, at least) that will take you as deeply into the *mystery* of living the Christian life as this one does.

Christian life is a mystery: the mystery of sharing in the divine life of God. You can't really experience Christianity until you have some awareness of *living on the level of God*. And this is an experience you keep growing into all of your life.

Mystery is the name of the game. A *mystery* is "a truth that invites endless exploration." God is a mystery; you don't know God until you get some idea of the mystery of what and who he is.

So, yes, this book will take you into mystery. But it will do it so easily, so simply, that it won't hurt at all.

INTRODUCTION
Growing Closer to God

To grow into deeper levels of intimacy with God, we need to know different ways of praying. Praying is all about loving. And loving depends on knowing. Prayer is endless exploration into the mystery of God.

The levels of intimacy with God correspond to the levels of intimacy we have with people. It is very simple. There are five levels and ways of praying that parallel five different ways we choose to communicate with people. Let's take a look at them.

Just Words
The first degree of intimacy is the level of relationship we have with people we only talk to in clichés, "pat phrases." We pass someone in the hall or on the street and say, "Hi! How you doin'?"

When we say this, we aren't really asking how the person is doing. Nor do we care. If he or she started to tell us, we would get impatient. We aren't paying attention to what the words mean. We are just using them to say that we notice the other person is there.

The Ngama tribe in Chad, Africa, is more honest. Their greeting is just "Mo doi"—"I see your head." And the answer is "Nel dom," "It pleases my head." The word "head" stands for "person." The

1

greeter is just saying, "I notice you." And the one greeted answers, "I'm glad you do." They say what they mean.

This first level—relationship restricted to communication in pat phrases—is not much. But it is better than ignoring people. This is the level of intimacy we have with God when we say vocal prayers— memorized prayers or prayers we read out of a book—without really paying attention or meaning what we say. For example, we make the Sign of the Cross as if we were brushing flies off our face; or we rattle off "Ourfatherwhoartinheavenhallowedbethyname…" without thinking of what we are saying. All we are really doing when we "say our prayers" like this is acknowledging that God exists. If this is our only level of communication with God, it isn't much. Still, it is better than nothing.

So yes, *say your prayers.* But make them more than pat phrases. Try to pay attention to the words and grow into meaning personally what they say.

Just Information

The second level of intimacy is the relationship we have with people with whom we share *information.* We ask a co-worker which team won the ball game, or an older person to tell us about World War II, or we ask directions from a stranger on the street. Even this establishes a kind of relationship, expresses a certain trust.

We get on this level with God when we want to know more *about* him. We enjoy learning interesting facts about the life and times of Jesus. Or, going deeper, we study theology for "academic knowledge"—or even to teach or preach to others in an educational

2

way, without necessarily revealing any personal relationship with God on our part or calling for it from others.

There are certain prayers we say, or can say, that mainly just remind us of what the church teaches. We can, for example, recite the *Profession of Faith* at Mass without any sense at all of declaring our personal choice to believe. We can even listen to the words of the Eucharistic Prayer with attention, trying to grasp their meaning, but without realizing that they are our own words that we are saying, that the presider is just pronouncing out loud in our name. This is a level of participation at Mass that may be higher than average. But we are still just taking in information.

All the above is good. It shows a certain amount of faith in Jesus, a real interest in him and a trust that there is something about him worth knowing.

Don't knock this. If we knew more about Jesus, we would love him more. If we knew more about what the church teaches, we would appreciate our religion more. Many people have left the church and are leaving it today for lack of accurate information.

That is why it is important to seek information. Does the church really teach those things you find objectionable? Does the interpretation of God's law that you got from your pastor, bishop, or the last priest you went to confession to really reflect the true mind and heart of the church? The mind and heart of God? How are you to know, if they are your only source of information?

So talk to other priests, or to laypersons, who seem to be holy and happy living the Christian life. Read books. Read the lives of saints and the writings of involved Christians. Do what we used to call "spiritual reading." Look up what the church herself says, what she has said in worldwide councils and some of the encyclicals—worldwide letters—of the popes. Begin by reading the sixteen short documents of Vatican II (the second council of the church to be held in Vatican City; it met from 1962-1965). And above all, *go to the source*. Read Scripture.

You can be sure of one thing: if something is contrary to the word of God, it is not the real teaching of the Catholic Church, even if it is the teaching of many *in* the church. But how will you know what Jesus said if all you get is other people's predigested interpretations of it? Let Jesus himself speak to you. Read the Bible. If something is confusing, use the explanations of respected Scripture scholars that are available in serious books that are not just echoing current positions. Read what the experts say.[1]

Dealing with Opinions

On the third level of intimacy, we share *opinions* with others. This is to reveal something of a more personal nature. Our opinions are not just abstract facts. They are judgments we have made that reveal a lot about us: our level of intelligence and education, even our prejudices and values. We don't share our opinions with just anybody. We "watch what we say" around strangers. We only speak freely with people we think we can trust.

To ask someone's opinion, or to share our own, is a significant step into deeper personal relationship. It is not to be taken for granted.

Once, while trying to explain the Christian understanding of love to a group of Ngama men in Chad (where women and men did not, at that time, discuss things together), I asked: "Do you ever ask your wife's opinion about anything?"

There was a long silence. Then one man spoke: "I paid more for my oxen than I did for my wife, and I never ask my oxen's opinion about anything." Another summed it up: "I don't ask my wife's opinion about anything because, in my opinion, my wife doesn't know anything."

We laugh. But when I told this story during a retreat in the United States, one woman remarked: "So what's the difference between men over there and men over here?" Again, we can laugh. But it is not a laughing matter when husbands and wives do not probe each other's minds—and reveal their own—in deep discussion about all sorts of matters. What does it say about the respect they have or do not have for each other? About how well they want to know each other?

Nor is it a laughing matter when pastors do not ask their parishioners' opinions about doctrine, liturgy, and the effect that ministry in the parish is having on people. Or when the pope does not consult the bishops, or the bishops their priests and (very emphatically "and") the laypeople about the way things are going in the church. What does non-consultation say about the pope's attitude toward the bishops, the bishops' attitude toward priests and laity alike, and the pastor's attitude toward the other members of the parish community, of which he is also a member?

Being pastor does not put one above or outside of the community. It is just one ministry among others. As St. Paul says:

> There are varieties of services, but the same Lord; and there are varieties of activities, but it is the same God who activates all of them in everyone. To each is given the manifestation of the Spirit for the common good. (1 Corinthians 12:5–7)

We are all one team. We need to play as one. This is a matter of relationship. If we don't want to know others' opinions, then we do not want to have any real relationship with them as persons. We either do not respect them as having any opinions worth hearing, or we just don't care about being in union of mind and will and heart with them, even concerning things we are involved in doing together. We want a "master and slave" relationship. Not *koinonia*. Not "community." Not "communion in the Holy Spirit."

Grow

Many, many Catholics are comfortable being "slaves," and many in the clergy and hierarchy are very willing to oblige them. The laity say, "Just give us the rules." And the clergy say, "Here they are; obey them." No opinions change sides.

Relationships are determined by *interaction*. The kind and level of our interaction with one another determines the kind and level of relationship we have with each other. Is it purely professional? Just social? Rigidly hierarchical? The relationship of masters and slaves?[2]

Apply this to our relationship with Jesus. What kind of relationship—that is, what kind of *interaction*—do we want to have with him? Do we want to explore what he thinks about things? Do we want to enter into more personal relationship with him by reading and thinking about the words he spoke (and is still speaking to us) in the Gospels? Or do we just want to learn his rules and leave it at that?

Jesus was explicit in saying he does not want slaves, or even servants. He said, "I do not call you servants any longer, because the servant does not know what the master is doing; but I have called you *friends*, because I have *made known to you* everything that I have heard from my Father" (John 15:15).

When we accept to share our opinions with others, and invite others to share their opinions with us, we have made a great step forward in personal relationship and intimacy. We make this same great step forward in our relationship with God when we begin looking into his opinions.

An "opinion" is defined as "the view somebody takes about a certain issue, especially when it is based solely on personal judgment."[3] The fact that, in God's case, his opinions are always true does not mean they are any less his opinions. To be interested in "the view Jesus takes about a certain issue"—or about all issues—is to enter into a higher and deeper level of personal relationship with him, especially when we are aware that his opinions are based "on his personal judgment." Jesus' opinions reveal to us the personal mind and heart of God. They help us to know Jesus and God as a person.

In the Second Vatican Council the bishops declared that the church:

> earnestly and especially urges all the Christian faithful…to learn by frequent reading of the divine Scriptures the "excellent knowledge of Jesus Christ" (see Philippians 3:8). "For ignorance of the Scriptures is ignorance of Christ" (St. Jerome). Therefore, they should gladly put themselves in touch with the sacred text itself, whether it be through the liturgy…or through devotional reading, or through instructions suitable for the purpose and other aids which, in our time…are commendably available everywhere [for example, Scripture study groups].

And let them remember that prayer should accompany the reading of Sacred Scripture, so that God and humans may talk together; for "we speak to Him when we pray; we hear Him when we read the divine saying" (St. Ambrose). (On Divine Revelation, no. 25)

To take Jesus' opinions seriously, we should *argue* with him. We are not coming to grips with his mind if we read something he says that we find hard to accept and just say, "Well, he is God, so it has to be true," and leave it at that. To do him justice, we have to challenge what he says, make clear to ourselves and to him what it is that rubs us the wrong way. If we put into words our objections to what he says, we give him a chance to answer. For example, Jesus said:

Do not resist an evildoer. But if anyone strikes you on the right cheek, turn the other also; and if anyone wants to sue you and take your coat, give your cloak as well; and if anyone forces you to go one mile, go also the second mile. Give to everyone who begs from you, and do not refuse anyone who wants to borrow from you. (Matthew 5:39–42)

We are not about to take this seriously! It is too farfetched. But we don't want to argue with God, so we just say, "Yeah, yeah," and ignore it, which means we ignore Jesus. We treat him like the people we don't consider worth arguing with. When we argue with God, we need to say at the beginning that we know he is right. But if we don't understand *why* he is right, we aren't really going to live by what he says. Not fully. Not wholeheartedly. At most we will obey like servants or slaves, not act in union of mind and will and heart with Jesus like partners. Like friends.

So argue. Ask all the questions. And try to answer them. The disciples didn't understand everything Jesus said either. So he promised them before he died:

> I have said these things to you while I am still with you. But the Advocate, the Holy Spirit, whom the Father will send in my name, will teach you everything, and remind you of all that I have said to you. Peace I leave with you; my peace I give to you. (John 14:25–27)

We let God share his opinions with us when we read and reflect on Scripture with an inquiring mind. When we *meditate.* Whenever anything Jesus says disturbs our peace, we should ask the Holy Spirit to help us figure it out. Then try. Learning the mind and heart of God is a gradual process. We grow into it. How? We enter into prayer. We meditate.

Expressing Emotions

The fourth level of intimacy—and of prayer—is to express our emotions.

We are not talking here about the emotions we can't hide, as when we blow up at someone and show impatience or anger. We are talking about the act of *choosing* to reveal to another—or others—not just what we think but what we feel.

We like to believe that what we think is just objective truth, that when we express an opinion, no one should take it personally, as if we were saying something about ourselves or them as persons.

We like to think of ourselves as detached observers who are simply "calling a spade a spade."

This isn't true, of course, but there is enough truth in it to let us think we are not making ourselves naked to the world in expressing what we think. Not so when we express our feelings.

What we call "spontaneity"—just being ourselves without reserve, without "monitoring" everything we say and how we say it—is really a choice to *give up control*.

Not completely, of course. We should never do that. But when we spontaneously express what we are feeling (laughing and crying with others, giving impulsive hugs and kisses, jumping up yelling when our team makes a touchdown, or even making excited gestures as we talk)—when we do any of this, we are giving up some measure of conscious control. We reveal ourselves in an "unedited" way. We just "do what comes naturally" and so let "the real us" appear.

To do this—to relinquish control and express physically and visibly what we are feeling—is to enter into another level of intimacy with others. It is to lower our guard, let down some barriers; it is, to some extent, to become "naked" to those we are with.

Naked is the way humans were with each other before sin entered the world. Scripture says Adam and Eve "were both naked, and were not ashamed." They had nothing to be ashamed of, nothing they were afraid to let others see. But after their sin, "then the eyes of both were opened, and they knew that they were naked; and they sewed fig leaves together and made loincloths for themselves" (Genesis 2:25—3:7).

Every person born into the world lives through this experience. When we are toddlers, we run around naked, acting out whatever we feel. No one has ever hurt us. But the first day we go to school, this begins to change. If we feel lonely on the playground and begin to cry, others may stand around and call us "sissy." We learn it is not always safe to express our emotions. We are "putting on clothes."

Later, as teenagers, without thinking about it, we express our opinion about something in a group. Everyone makes fun of us; ridicules us; says we are "stupid." We learn not to say what we think. We are putting on more clothes.

By the time we are adults, we walk around in a full suit of armor, hiding our true selves behind all sorts of defenses and reserves. We are careful about "opening up." We know that if we reveal ourselves in the slightest, open up the smallest chink in our armor, someone might stab us through it.

When Jesus came to heal and reverse the sin of Adam and Eve, he did not restore the primitive nakedness of Eden. Until all reach the "perfection of love" in the total mutual forgiveness and acceptance of the "wedding banquet of the Lamb," sin is still a fact of our environment. It would be naïve to "wear our heart on our sleeve." If we reveal ourselves to everyone, we can and will be hurt. Jesus knew that. But he let himself be stripped naked on the cross. His heart was revealed to the whole world. We stabbed him through it. And since then his heart has been open to everyone who lives.

Instead of returning us to the primitive nakedness of Eden, Jesus told us to clothe ourselves in the white robe of the wedding feast. A wedding dress is something one puts on as a promise to take it off. It is a pledge of nakedness. The physical nakedness of marriage is a pledge to be naked to each other in mind and heart and soul.

Implicit in this is the promise of spontaneity. Married couples will never know themselves completely, never come to total union of mind and will and—especially—of heart, if they do not release all reserves and abandon themselves without restraint to passionate self-expression. This reaches a height in sexual surrender.

Are those who marry so naïve that they think they will never hurt each other? No, their nakedness is not the nakedness of Adam and Eve, free of all fears in the Garden of Eden. It is the nakedness of Jesus on the cross, as they deliver themselves up in love, knowing their vulnerability will open them to wounds that will be inflicted, but determined to persevere through every hurt, never to close their hearts to each other in any degree, until, as Jesus proved it could, *amor vincit omnia*. Love—not human love alone, but their love made divine—"conquers all."

This is sublime, but true. And it is no less true if we seem to go from the sublime to the ridiculous by coming down to the nuts and bolts of something as simple (and challenging) as—singing at Mass!

In ninety-nine percent of the cases, all the reasons people give for not singing at Mass are rationalizations. Just excuses.

"I can't sing." (You don't sing "Happy Birthday" at parties?)

"I don't know the words." (You can't remember "*Al-le-lu-ia*"?)

The real reason is just plain fear. Fear of joining in. Fear of "losing" themselves in communal celebration. Fear of looking like they are involved (teenagers). Fear of expressing emotion. Some who do sing don't really "enter into" the hymn; they sing it as if the words mean nothing to them.

People stop going to Mass because they say it is "dead." But when they did go, what did they do to liven it up? If they just stood there like statues while the church was celebrating the redemption of the world, no wonder they "got nothing out of it." They put nothing into it.

The reason we sometimes don't "get anything" out of prayer is because we don't understand the level of communication God wants to have with us. Or we are afraid to enter into it.

To communicate with God about emotional issues requires emotional self-expression. We said above that married couples will never know themselves completely, never come to total union of mind and will and—especially—of heart, if they do not release all reserves and abandon themselves to spontaneous, passionate self-expression. The same is true of union with God. What are we talking about? What are the nuts and bolts here?

In El Paso, Texas, after six years of seminary training in prayer and the spiritual life, I saw a young Mexican-American praying before a statue of Our Lady of Guadalupe with his arms stretched out in the form of a cross. I said to myself, "I wish I could pray like that."

He was praying with his whole body. That showed he was praying with his heart. He was not only *expressing* what he felt; he was *experiencing* it. This is a law of nature: *what you do not express you will not experience.* At least, not fully.

If you do not *express* any emotional response to God, you will not *experience* any. You will have a very "formal" and "proper" relationship with God as Creator and Lord, but you won't experience passionate love, or ever sense that you care about him.

Try these nuts and bolts. When you get out of bed in the morning, if you are alone, kneel down and put your forehead on the floor. Adore God with your body and see what effect it has on your soul. Say the Our Father like this.

Then say the following prayer kneeling with your arms

stretched out in the form of a cross. With your arms extended in "self-oblation," express the passionate offering of yourself to him: "*Lord, I give you my body. Live this day with me, live this day in me, live this day through me.*" (You'll hear this prayer a lot as we journey through this book—I call it the WIT Prayer: W-ith, I-n, T-hrough.)

Scripture tells us that when King David brought the ark of God up to Jerusalem "with rejoicing," he stripped off his clothes and "danced before the LORD with all his might" dressed only in a linen apron.

When his wife Michal saw him "leaping and dancing before the LORD," she "despised him in her heart," and said to him sarcastically, "How the king of Israel has honored himself today! Uncovering himself before the eyes of his servants' maids, as any worthless person might shamelessly uncover himself!"

David answered her, "It was before the LORD, who chose me as prince over the people of the LORD, that I have danced. I will make myself yet more contemptible than this, and I will be abased in my own eyes; but by the maids of whom you have spoken, by them I shall be held in honor."

The story ends, "And Michal the daughter of Saul had no child to the day of her death" (2 Samuel 6:12–23).

So let's be real. How would you feel about someone who joined the procession at Mass, dancing wildly to the Entrance Hymn as the presiding priest enters? Wouldn't you say that was stupid? What if everybody in church started dancing? Would you join in? Or would you join Michal in "despising" them? Maybe this is one of the reasons why so many of our parishes have trouble reproducing themselves.

If you do nothing else, *get in touch with your feelings as you pray.*

There is a form, or level, of prayer we call "affective prayer." It is not "meditation," understood as going from question to question, thought to thought, until we can respond with a decision to something we have chosen to focus on. In "affective prayer" we are not going anywhere; we are already there. We have seen what we need to see; now we are just "resting" in it. Contemplating it. Feeling it. Absorbing it and absorbed in it. Adoring. Wishing. Longing. Loving. The "body language" of "affective prayer" is mostly just stillness. That too can be an expression of emotion.

Sharing "Peak Experiences"

We reach the highest level of intimacy in sharing our "peak experiences" with another. "Sharing" here could mean either just revealing or participating together in the same experience. This is to share with others the deepest level of our self-knowledge.

> *Psychologist Abraham Maslow describes peak experiences as especially joyous and exciting moments in life, involving sudden feelings of intense happiness and well-being, wonder and awe, and possibly also involving an awareness of transcendental unity or knowledge of higher truth (as though perceiving the world from an altered, and often vastly profound and awe-inspiring, perspective). They usually come on suddenly and are often inspired by deep meditation, intense feelings of love, exposure to great art or music, or the overwhelming beauty of nature.[4]*

What would we call peak experiences in the spiritual life? And how do they affect our prayer life, our conscious interaction with God?

The answer is: "our *key mystical experiences.*" We need to know: 1. that we have had them; 2. what they are; 3. how we should let them help us on the nuts-and-bolts level of our daily dealings with God.

Maslow claimed that "virtually everyone has a number of peak experiences in the course of their life. But often such experiences either go unrecognized, misunderstood or are simply taken for granted. In so-called 'non-peakers', peak experiences are somehow resisted and suppressed" (Wikipedia, "Peak Experiences").

Jesuit John English says the same about our deepest religious experiences, which we should not hesitate to call mystical experiences. These need not be particular moments of intellectual enlightenment or emotional realization. Each may be spread out over the course of years. But there is a definite "before and after" during which we recognize that we have experienced something that has profoundly affected our awareness. But often such experiences go unrecognized. As with Maslow's "non-peakers," in those who claim they have had no mystical experiences, recognition of them "is somehow resisted and suppressed."

Why? Probably because we were trained to think that only special people like the saints have mystical experiences. We grew up thinking it would be something extraordinary to actually experience in any way the mystery of our divine life and of God's divine interaction with us—as if God, who created us in his own image as Trinity, and whose life is a constant ongoing interaction between Father, Son, and Spirit, would not interact with us who are sharing his life!

We need to be *aware* of his interaction with us: to think back, to remember and identify the moments when some realization about God, or experience of his action on us or in the world, had a significant or life-changing good effect on us.

This could be something that happened over a period of time: something we saw in our parents' relationship with God that we knew was true. It could be a teacher or period during our education that made religion real to us. Perhaps a friendship brought us closer to God.

We could find it by just identifying certain attitudes, certain responses of faith, hope, or love that were so strong and clear in us that they had to come from God, something we knew was a gift, and that was a determining element in our personal relationship with God. Or it could be a special moment of interaction and response—a decision or choice that we know now, and probably knew then, was specifically influenced by God.

These are not moments we share lightly with others. But when we do, it brings our relationship to a new and deeper level.

When I was in Africa with the French Jesuits, they asked me to be an "ecumenical bridge" to the American missionaries there. So I called on the Protestant pastor.

When he told me he was Baptist, I asked, "Southern Baptist?"

"No," he said, "the Southern Baptists are modernists!"

"You are a Northern Baptist?"

"Of course not. The Northern Baptists are agnostics."

"Then what kind of Baptist are you?"

He answered, "I am a *Regular* Baptist."

Then I knew. Lester was about as fundamentalist as you could get.

In our discussions, that was a stone wall. Once I stayed at his house until midnight trying to convince Lester that we were not worshiping idols when we prayed in front of statues and crucifixes. "We don't adore the images or the wood of the cross."

"You kneel down before them. That is to adore them."

I got nowhere by insisting that we knelt to pray to God and that the images were just to help us focus on him.

Then one day I asked, "Lester, how did you get to Africa?"

He answered by telling me about his experience of being called by God. Then I told him about my experience of being called by God. When I finished, he looked at me and said, "David, but you're *saved*! You're the first Catholic priest I've ever met who's saved!"

"Lester," I said, "I'm the only Catholic priest you ever talked to." (Certainly the only one who ever shared a "peak experience" with him!)

Then we each described when and how Jesus first became real to us. Lester was "saved" in a moment of conversion, during a Baptist revival. He turned away from sin and gave his life to God. I told him there was no such dramatic moment of conversion in my life, but that I grew up in a home where God was unostentatiously taken for granted, and Jesus had always been real to me.

Lester's wife said that was her experience. "I can't tell you at what moment I was saved. Like you, I just always knew he was there."

From that moment on, we could talk about anything. Doctrines were no longer a problem. We were brothers and sister in Christ, and the same Spirit was working in all three of us. Our differences were a matter of words. We could get past them.

Until we know how another has interacted personally with God, we do not know who we are dealing with. And until we get in touch with our own experience of interacting with God—deeply and personally—we do not know how to deal with ourselves.

We learn who we are only when we realize how God sees us. For that we need to remember, to identify, to "own" the history of his communication with us, and our response.

On the nuts-and-bolts level of practical use, Father John English teaches that the art (and gift) of "discerning," of recognizing the inspirations and movements of the Holy Spirit in our hearts, is easier if we have put ourselves in touch with our own "unique experience of receiving consolation from God."[5]

To know whether God is speaking to us now, we compare what we are experiencing now to the way God communicated with us in those special, key moments when we clearly recognized his voice.

God deals with each of us in an individual way. With Peter, Jesus could be rough, as when he told him: "Get out of my sight, you devil. You are an obstacle in my path!" (Matthew 16:23). If Jesus ever spoke to me like that, I would crumble! So he speaks to me gently. That is one way I "recognize his voice." So it will help if we each go back over our history of hearing God's voice, getting in touch with the particular style and "tone of voice" that he uses when speaking to us. This helps us identify him.

We were made for communication with God. That is the purpose and key of our existence. We can communicate with him in different ways and on different levels. Each level brings us into deeper intimacy with him: into deeper knowledge and love of God, which are inseparable from deeper knowledge and—yes—love of ourselves.

To "know God," and ourselves as shaped by our relationship with him—this is the purpose, the goal, and the fulfillment of human life. To simply rest in *awareness* of who God is and who we are is the deepest level of prayer.

So, get to know God as deeply and passionately as God wants to know you. These simple nuts and bolts are a simple, practical, and profitable way to get started. God calls us to great things, and God trusts us to carry them out!

The WIT PRAYER

The first nut and bolt you need in order to put your spiritual life together is to say the WIT prayer every morning—as soon as you wake up, before you even open your eyes—and keep saying it all day long. What is the WIT prayer?

> *Lord, I give you my body.*
> *Live this day* with *me,*
> *live this day* in *me,*
> *live this day* through *me.*

If you like, you can add, "Let me think with your thoughts, and speak with your words, and act as your body on earth."

Then all day long, before everything you do, keep repeating it: "Lord, do this *with* me, do this *in* me, do this *through* me."

That alone will transform your life. You don't believe me? Start doing it and see. This prayer will keep you *aware* of the mystery of your existence. What is that mystery, and why is it so important to stay aware of it?

You Can't Get There from Here

Everyone knows the story of the Irishman trying to tell a tourist how to reach a little shrine out in the country. After several complicated attempts the guide finally concluded: "You can't get there from here."

The spiritual life is like that. You can't get to the "fullness of life" from just anywhere. You have to know where you are to start with—and where you are going.

Before you can be clear about what you want to be, you have to know what you are right now. Most people don't. The truth about what you are may shock you. The simple truth is that when you were baptized you *became Christ.*

This is not the way you habitually think of yourself? Not a definition you can accept, or use to describe yourself to others? Does it sound far out? Well, believe it or not, these are the words of St. Augustine (died 430 A.D.), quoted by Pope John Paul II in the first chapter of his letter *The Splendor of Truth,* and then included in the *Catechism of the Catholic Church*, paragraph 795. Augustine said, speaking to the baptized:

> *Let us rejoice then and give thanks that we have become not only Christians, but Christ himself. Do you understand and grasp, brethren, God's grace toward us? Marvel and rejoice: we have become Christ! (Catechism of the Catholic Church, no. 795)*

This is the first mystery of baptism and its first promise: a *new identity.* Jesus taught us to begin our prayer by owning it: "Our *Father, who art in heaven..."* It is the first thing we celebrate at Mass, whose *Introductory Rites* not only introduce the eucharistic celebration, but also introduce us to ourselves, to the mystery of who we are as Christians. The "grace of our Lord Jesus Christ" is the favor of *sharing in the divine life of God* through incorporation into Christ as members of his body. We begin Mass by identifying ourselves—and all those assembled with us—as people who have *become Christ*, and for that reason are children of the Father.

We can't marvel and rejoice that we have "become Christ" unless we believe it. And we can't believe a shocking statement like this without some explanation. So here it comes. But before going into it, we should realize that by saying the WIT prayer all day long, we will grow painlessly into understanding this mystery while hardly noticing it. It is *so* easy.

So why is it so shocking to say we have *become Christ*? Because we think we've got the answer when we define ourselves as human beings. Or by what we do. These definitions are incomplete. They don't begin to embrace the totality of our real identity.

What Am I?

Believe it or not, every time you pray the Our Father you are speaking your real identity out loud. You've said it over and over again, perhaps without realizing what the words mean. Take another look. "*Our Father, who art in heaven...*"—If God is your father, what does that make you?

It makes you a real son or daughter of God, "with all the rights and privileges thereof." That is how God sees you. That is how you should see him and interact with him. That can change your whole life!

According to our faith, there is only one Son of God: the Second Person of the Blessed Trinity, God the Son, who took on flesh in

Jesus Christ. The only way we can become real sons or daughters of the Father is to become *filii in Filio.* This is an ancient, traditional expression in the church that means "sons [and daughters] *in the Son*" (saying it in Latin makes it official!). We become children of the Father by becoming the body, the real body, of Jesus the "only Son of God." By *becoming Christ.*[6]

If you ask yourself, "What am I?" answer yourself: "I am a living, breathing offspring of God! I am a divine member of the family of God himself, because I have *become Christ,* who is the Father's only Son. In Christ I am a real son, a real daughter of God! God is not just my Creator. He is my Father!"

When you hear at the beginning of Mass, "*May the grace of our Lord Jesus Christ be with you,*" you are hearing the same thing.

But what is "grace"? (Now is your chance to pin that one down.) "Grace" simply means "favor." What favor? The favor of *sharing in the divine life of God.* That's pretty simple, isn't it? But if you share in God's own divine life, you are divine. How does that make you feel? Won't that "jump start" the Mass for you?

Many times you have heard Saint Paul saying in the Mass readings that God chose him to make known "the glory of *this mystery, which is Christ in you,* the hope of glory." And you have heard Paul's description of himself, which is really a description of everyone who has received "the grace of our Lord Jesus Christ" by baptism: "It is no longer I who live, but *it is Christ who lives in me.*" Now, if we have not "become Christ," and are not sharing in God's divine life by being "in Christ," we are not divine. But we *have* "become Christ," and we *do* share in his divine life, and "in him" we are divine. No wonder we celebrate the "grace of our Lord Jesus Christ"!

So let's be clear from the beginning: the only way you can start off on the path that leads to the "fullness of life" is to recognize that the life you are talking about is *divine* life, and you already have it. You want to grow into the fullness of what you already are. You have already *become Christ* by baptism—that is what you are. Now you want to live Christ's life, his divine life, to the full.

That is what spiritual growth is all about. The best way to start is to begin saying the WIT prayer.

Christ Growing in Us

In baptism, we not only became Christ, but Christ became *us* by taking us to be his real body. *With* us—and *in* us and *through* us—Jesus is living his own life in partnership with us who are sharing it with him.

The word *partnership* gives us the key. Partners in a business have equal voice. They make all their decisions together. Their employees may or may not understand what they are doing or why; their job is just to carry out orders. But the partners—in order to cooperate, to really work together as partners—have to be thinking alike, seeing things the same way, wanting the same things, agreeing with each other, and acting as one in the decisions they make in running the business.

That is the way we are partners with Jesus in the business of living his divine life on earth as human beings who are his body. Jesus said, "I do not call you servants any longer, because the servant does not know what the master is doing; but *I have called you friends, because I have made known to you everything* that I have heard from my Father" (John 15:15). Jesus doesn't just do in us and through us whatever he pleases. He cannot act in "partnership" with us unless we are cooperating, working together with him in everything he wants to do.[7]

Paul wrote that the church will only come to maturity when all her members have become so united with Jesus and each other "in faith and in the knowledge of God's Son" that they "*form that perfect man* who is *Christ come to full stature*" (Ephesians 4:13). The church will be fully what it should be only when Jesus has become fully what he wants to be in the humans who are his body on earth.

Jesus cannot speak *in* us, and *through* our words, unless we know what we are saying and want to say it *with* him. Our bodies are not just loudspeakers for Jesus; what people hear us saying has to be something we ourselves are saying in unison with him, our own self-expression. For Jesus and us to be speaking with one voice, we have to be one with him in mind and will and heart. But if this is to happen, we have to understand what we are doing with him and really want to do it. And he has to "make it known" to us.

That is something we have to grow into. We aren't born with it. We are born with something called "original sin." Let's look at that a little more closely.

The "Vulture of Culture"

Most of what humans do is the fruit of cultural conditioning. We act out of attitudes, values, priorities, fears, and compulsions that are programmed into us from the day we start interacting with other human beings—that is, from the moment we are born. No one escapes the influence, good and bad, of the "culture"—which means everything we learn from mixing with other people. Repeat: this is both good and bad.

Since all the people we deal with have been influenced—and infected—by their culture, and by others who were influenced and infected by their culture before that, going back to the beginnings of the human race, we are all infected from birth with attitudes and values that oppose the attitudes and values of Jesus within us. St. Paul himself experienced this. Yes, he said, "it is no longer I who live; *it is Christ who lives in me.*" But he also said:

> *I do not understand my own actions....For I do not do the good I want, but the evil I do not want is what I do....For I delight in the law of God in my inmost self, but I see in my members another law at war with the law of my mind, making me captive to the law of sin that dwells in my members....So then, with my mind I am a slave to the law of God, but with my flesh I am a slave to the law of sin." (Romans 7:15–25)*

Even in Paul, Christ was still "growing to full stature." We have to grow, and let Jesus grow in us, by working to "put on the Lord Jesus Christ, making no provision for the flesh, to gratify its desires." To "live our lives in a manner worthy of the gospel of Christ," we have to "let the same mind be in us that was in Christ Jesus."

Ready, Set...

What we need to be clear about here, before we set out on our journey, is the *goal*. We have to know what we are aiming at, what we are trying to become.

And since we know at the starting point what we already are— that we have *become Christ* by baptism—we know that the goal is to become Christ completely. *We must "grow up in every way into him who is the head," into the "fullness of Christ."*

In a nutshell, our goal is to become holy. And *holy* means *being in union with Jesus Christ.* We want to grow into perfect union—of mind and will and heart—with Jesus Christ. We want to be so one with him that he can do whatever he wants to do—*with us, in us,* and *through us*—in everything we say and do. This is "life to the full." This is "the perfection of love."

So let's go for it. Start saying the WIT prayer!

...Go!

To begin, say the WIT prayer all day long: "Lord, do this *with* me, do this *in* me, do this *through* me." Say it when you wake up, when you get out of bed, when you step out of your room, when you leave your house, when you get into your car or walk into your work-place, when you sit down at your desk, when you open a drawer or turn on your computer, when you pick up the telephone, and every time you start a conversation or someone starts one with you.

Say it when you go home, fix yourself a drink, or turn on the television. Say it when you kiss your spouse or play with your children. Say it when you write a letter or pick up a book to read. Say it when you clean your house or mow the lawn—say it *all day long!* Make it a habit. Say it until saying it becomes second nature to you. Say the words until they are implanted in your mind. Until they settle into your heart. Until they become the abiding stance of your will. Don't do anything without saying, "Lord, do this *with* me, do this *in* me, do this *through* me."

Why is this so important? Because you want always to be

conscious that you have *become Christ*. Nothing you do is just you acting, just your own action. You act in partnership with Jesus. He wants to act *with* you, *in* you, and *through* you in everything you do. This is what it means to be a Christian—that is, to *be Christ*.

To grow in the Christian life, we have to be *aware* of what we are. To *experience* anything, we have to be conscious of it. And it is only by experiencing the Christian life that we will appreciate it enough to want to grow in it.

The psalm says, "Taste and see that the Lord is good." If you don't taste you won't see. And if you don't see (let's be honest) you won't believe. And if you don't believe enough to *act*, you will not really take in what you do see. So taste. That's what keeps you eating. Tasting the "bread of life" will make you keep coming back for more.

We say in the Our Father, "Give us this day our *daily* bread." It is a daily meal—and one that lasts all day! Jesus said: "I am the *bread of life*...the living bread that came down from heaven. Whoever eats of this bread will live forever" (John 6:51).

Is that enough reason to say the WIT prayer?

If you do, it will keep you *aware* all day long that your life is a *mystery* of living on the level of God. That your life is divine; that you are divine; that you are never alone; that Jesus is acting *with* you, *in* you, and *through* you in everything you do. That you have entered into *partnership* with him, and he with you, to live one life together.

Cultivating this awareness is the first step along the path of spiritual growth. The first phase of growing into the fullness of life is to keep yourself *aware* of what you are and what you are trying to become. So work at it. Say the WIT prayer all day long.

Putting the Nut on the Bolt

You have to do one more thing before you can start. You have to choose a "gimmick."

What will remind you to say the WIT prayer all day long? It isn't just going to happen simply because you decide to do it. You will forget. That is normal.

So, until saying the WIT prayer all day long becomes a habit, something you do automatically, you have to use something to remind you, a "gimmick." The gimmick has to be something that works for *you*. It has to be a nut that fits the bolt you are using.

This means you have to find a reminder that fits your mentality, that fits into your lifestyle. What will work for you? A handkerchief on your doorknob that reminds you every time you walk through the door? Something on your telephone? Or your credit card? Your car keys? A pipe cleaner on your steering wheel? A rubber band around your wrist?

Can you make WIT part of your password? Your screen saver? Hang a crucifix on your whiskey bottle or a medal on your corkscrew? Put your TV remote in the arms of a statue? Make your watch beep you every hour? Program your cell phone to ring by saying, "WIT, WIT, WIT"? (When people ask you what that is all about, teach them to use the prayer!)

Make it a bumper sticker, an emblem on your tee shirt. Some inspired Evangelicals made WWJD popular (google it). Follow their lead. WIT says the same thing, only with more theology.

This chapter supplies the bolt. But you have to find the nut that fits it for you.

Whether you look for it or not will tell you whether you are actually choosing to make this first step toward the fullness of life.

My suggestion? Do it now.

PUT *the* BIBLE
on YOUR PILLOW

So now you have your gimmick to remind you to say the WIT prayer. Great. Let's continue.

The second nut and bolt you need in order to grow into the fullness of life is to *get a Bible* and put it, not on a shelf or on the table by your bed, but *on your pillow.* The pillow is the secret.

You can't go to sleep with a Bible under your ear. Putting one on your pillow will guarantee that you pick it up once a day—more than most people do in a lifetime. And that will radically change your life. Again, please don't take my word for it. Start doing it and see.

You do have to make a promise, but one so easy to keep you will never have an excuse to break it. Promise God that when you pick up your Bible from your pillow you will never go to sleep without reading *one line.*

Does that sound ridiculous? Like "tokenism"? Why not a chapter? Because you wouldn't do it. Why not a paragraph, then? Because some nights you wouldn't do that either. Why not at least a complete sentence? The answer is that you want to make your promise so easy—so ridiculously easy—that it will never be too hard to keep it.

You come home from a New Year's Eve party at three in the

morning. After a while you figure out what that something bulky is under your ear that is blocking your sleep. You pick it up. What does it cost you to read *one line*?

If you open the Bible at random, you may read: "Be drunk, but not from wine" (Isaiah 29:9). You say, "Thank God it was bourbon," and go right to sleep!

If you just read one line, you have the satisfaction, the self-affirmation, of having kept your promise to God. You begin the New Year keeping your resolution.

If you begin and end every day keeping a promise to God, that is encouraging. You begin with a win and end with a victory. That is self-affirming. It motivates you to keep it up. *That* is the point of only promising to read one line.

The fact is, most nights you will read two or three lines, or at least a complete sentence. But don't promise it! Keep your promise so easy you will never have an excuse or a reason for not keeping it. Even if you stop reading in the middle of a sentence, you can say to God, "I have kept my promise!"

And God smiles and says to you, "You have. I am happy with you. Now go to sleep."

Bracket the Day

When you finish reading your one line, don't put the Bible on the table by your bed. You will not remember to pick it up again. Instead, put it on the floor, on top of your shoes. That way you can't get dressed without picking it up again. When you get up, read one more line and put the Bible back on your pillow.

If you do this, you will begin and end every day reading the word of God. You will be letting God speak at least a few words to you every morning and every night. That is more than ninety-nine percent of the world does, and perhaps it is more than you yourself are doing right now.

Remember the story of Naaman, commander of the army of the king of Aram. Although a Gentile, he went to Elisha the prophet, on the advice of a Jewish slave, to be cured of leprosy.

When Naaman came with his horses and chariots, and halted at the entrance of the prophet's house, Elisha sent a messenger to him, saying, "Go, wash in the Jordan seven times, and your flesh shall be restored."

This made Naaman angry. He went away, saying, "I thought that for me he would surely come out, and stand and call on the name of the LORD his God, and would wave his hand over the spot, and cure the leprosy! Are not the rivers of Damascus better than all the waters of Israel? Could I not wash in them, and be clean?" He turned and went away in a rage.

But his servants approached and said to him, "Father, if the prophet had commanded you to do something difficult, would you not have done it? How much more, when all he said to you was, 'Wash, and be clean'?"

So he went down and immersed himself seven times in the Jordan, according to the word of the man of God. His flesh was restored like the flesh of a young boy, and he was clean.

Is reading one line a night more of a token gesture than this? Will you refuse to do it because it is so easy?

This second step makes reading the Bible so easy so you will never have an excuse not to do it. And every time you keep your promise it will encourage you to persevere.

But look at what reading one line a night will do for you. First, since it is probably more than you are doing now, it will be progress. Second, reading just one line a night will "break the sound barrier" between you and the Bible. Many people are afraid to read the Bible. They never pick it up, because they think they won't understand it. Or they have been taught that reading the Bible is dangerous! That they might get into "private interpretation" and become Protestants! Previous generations of Catholics were actually trained this way, and nothing the church has said since has been able to get this idea out of—and Bible reading into—the Catholic culture. Just beginning to read one line a night will cure you of this prejudice. You will actually begin to enjoy it!

And be ready for God to ever so gently begin to raise the ante. (He's quite a negotiator!) For example, he may say to you, "Why not just have one cup of coffee with me?" Just read a little bit of the Bible for the time it takes you to calmly enjoy one cup of coffee—at home, or in the office. Do you have a better way to start your day?

A Mystical Experience

If you read just a bit of the Bible every day, sooner or later you will experience the second *promise* of baptism: the promise of *divine enlightenment*. This also is a mystical experience—the experience, the conscious awareness, of the mystery of God actually speaking to you, sharing with you the divine light of his own divine knowledge of truth.

This doesn't "feel" like a mystical experience. There is no sudden, blinding experience of illumination. It is too gradual for that.

It is like the experience of sitting in your kitchen before dawn, drinking coffee in the dark and talking with someone. At some moment you become aware that, without your noticing it, the sun has gradually risen. Now you can see. And you are not sure exactly when that began.

If you keep reading the Bible, one day (and it won't take long) you will realize that now you are seeing things more clearly than before. You are understanding better what you read, understanding your religion better, and with more appreciation. You will feel more in touch with yourself and with God, more aware of your relationship.

You won't know exactly when this happened or how. You probably won't associate it with any special insights you had into particular passages of Scripture. You will just know that you have begun to see better. And that it makes you happier.

You may even begin to feel a sort of affection for the actual book of the Bible. It may give you a good feeling just to look at it or pick it up. The Bible has begun to be like a friend.

Then you should acknowledge the truth: you are having a mystical experience. God is enlightening you. You aren't seeing more clearly just because you are smart. You are experiencing the fulfillment of Jesus' promise: "I have said these things to you while I am still with you. But the Advocate, the Holy Spirit, whom the Father will send in my name, will teach you everything, and remind you of all that I have said to you" (John 14:25–26).

If you do this, you will be able to accept as true, and receive with gratitude, what Jesus said about you—that, not only he, but *you "are the light of the world"* (read it for yourself: Matthew 5:14).

Only when you realize and accept that you, you yourself, are the "light of the world," will you do what Jesus intends for you to do: "Let your light *shine before others,* so that they may see your good works and *give glory to your Father* in heaven."

Then when you pray, "*Our Father…hallowed be thy name!*" you will know that you are actually "glorifying" the Father, making God more known and loved. You are able to do this because you know him yourself now, more than before.

The Liturgy of the Word at Mass will start to come alive for you. You will hear the readings in their context within the whole story. Your experience of God's intimate communication of his truth to you when you read his words privately will let you experience the truth of what the church says in the *General Instruction on the Roman Missal:* "When the Sacred Scriptures are read in the Church, *God himself speaks* to his people, and Christ, *present in his own word,* proclaims the Gospel" (no. 29). You will experience this for yourself.

All this will come about if you just put the Bible on your pillow and promise to read *one line* every night. Is that a good deal, or what?

Putting the Nut on the Bolt

So…are you going to do this? Make a decision, yes or no.

Socrates said, "The unexamined life is not worth living." Another Greek said *gnothi seauton*—"Know thyself"—and inscribed it in gold letters over the portico of the temple at Delphi. You need to know yourself. If there is not a Bible on your pillow when you go to bed tonight, you need to be aware of what you have decided and why. And what it tells you about yourself.

Unless you already read the Bible every day, and have a gimmick that keeps you doing it, the decision not to put a Bible on your pillow may mean that you are choosing not to take the next step along the path of spiritual growth. If that is what you are deciding, face it and measure the consequences.

Very few Christians take this second step. There are almost no real "disciples" of Jesus Christ on the face of the earth!

Does that sound negative? Extreme? Consider this: how many people do you personally know who lead lives *characterized* by reflection on the message of Jesus? The word "disciple" means *student*. Being a *follower* of Jesus does not make you a disciple. To be a disciple you have to be his *student*. Just the fact that you may have "learned your religion" when you were young, and may still be learning something from the preaching you hear on Sundays, is not enough to make you a "disciple," a "student" of Jesus Christ. For that you have to be learning from him now. And you have to be "signed up" for it—registered, enrolled. You have to have made a *commitment* to regular class attendance or to regular study of some sort.

How many Christians do you know who have done this? How many do you know who could point to a specific time of day when they "sit at the feet" of Jesus to learn from him? How many can honestly call themselves "students" of the words of Jesus? Can you? If not, this is your chance.

Reading one line a night may not be enough to make you a full-fledged disciple ("full-fledged" means "fully feathered," someone with wings enough to fly), but it does make you a registered student. It means you have signed up. You are showing up every day, if only for a few minutes. If you do that, Jesus will work you into more.

So are you going to do it? Do you have the nut that fits the bolt? Do you have a Bible, your own copy? Is it a cheap one? One you are not afraid to highlight and underline?

Where is it? Is there any reason why you can't put it on your pillow? (There might be one. A friend of mine put hers on her pillow and when she went to work her dog shredded it.) If you can't put it on your pillow, is there another place that will work for you just as well?

What is so practical about this second step is that you don't have to wonder and guess about whether you have made it or not. Just look on your bed. What you see there will tell you the truth.

My suggestion? Do it now.

The NUTS and BOLTS of PRAYER

When the Sacred Scriptures are read in the Church,
God himself speaks to his people,
and Christ, present in his own word, proclaims the Gospel....
For in the readings, God speaks to his people,
opening up to them the mystery of salvation...
and Christ himself is present
in the midst of the faithful through his word....[8]

The Bible is God's basic way of communicating with us. Reading the Bible is a way to get into a conversation with God. When we read it he talks to us. He speaks the written words to us as we read them. He expands on them; adds to them; explains what he has written.

He makes his words in the book personal to us by speaking them to us in particular, and with special affection. He lets us know and feel that he means them for us individually, that he is saying them to us. He goes into detail. He shows us how the words apply to our lives and lets us see special things he is asking of us that the words just suggest. God bounces off of the words to give us thoughts we could not have read in the words themselves, thoughts that may not even seem connected to them, but that the words have led us to.

The important thing about reading the Bible is not what God inspired someone to write a few thousand years ago. The important thing is what God is saying to us *now*. The written words are just a starting point. The conversation goes on from there. And we don't know where it might go.

Remember what Jesus said about being enlightened by his Holy Spirit: "The wind blows where it chooses, and you hear the sound of it, but you do not know where it comes from or where it goes. So it is with everyone who is born of the Spirit" (John 3:8). No telling what God may say to us when we read his words.

And don't fail to notice the "born of the Spirit" part. Understanding the Bible is not primarily a matter of brains. Remember that we are dealing with "mystery" here, the mystery of God's own mind and heart. We can't understand what God is saying about himself unless God gives us the special gift that we call "faith."

When Jesus said, "No one knows the Father but the Son," he was saying that we can only know God as he is by sharing in God's own life. To know the Father as our Father we must *be* the Son; that is, we have to have *become Christ* by being "born from above," born "of water and Spirit" by baptism.

When we live by the life of Jesus himself (which we call the "grace of our Lord Jesus Christ"), we share in Jesus' own act of knowing. That is what "faith" is. It is not we alone who read the Bible, but Jesus who is reading the words in us and catching us up in his own act of understanding them.

But remember: to act by grace is always to act in *partnership* with Jesus. He doesn't just put thoughts into our head; he joins in and takes part in our *act of thinking*. If we are thinking, Jesus can think *with us and in us and through us* as a partner, a co-thinker. His participation makes our act of thinking a divine as well as a human act. But the point is, for our thinking to be divine, it first of all has to be human. For us to get God's thoughts by reading the Bible, we have to *think*.[9]

The word we use for thinking about the Bible, or about anything else that can tell us about God, is *meditation*. It is a very simple process. The Mass should get us into it:

> *The Liturgy of the Word is to be celebrated in such a way as to promote meditation, in which...the word of God may be grasped by the heart.*[10]

The Nuts and Bolts of Meditation

There is nothing hard about meditating. You just follow the "three R's"—*Remembering, Reflecting, Responding*.

Remembering can also be *reading*. Writings are just recorded memories. The first step in meditating on the gospel is to call to mind, by reading or remembering, something that Jesus said or did. Confront it. Look at it. Don't let it just go in one ear and out the other. Take it seriously.

Reflecting is the way we take it seriously. We *think* about what the words mean, and especially about what they mean for us. This isn't hard.

Rudyard Kipling wrote a poem that gives us a practical guide for reflecting on Scripture (or anything else):

> *I keep six honest serving-men*
> *(They taught me all I knew);*

Their names are What and Why and When
And How and Where and Who.

We ask, "*What* did Jesus say or do here? *Why* did he say it or do it? *When* might it apply to my life? When could I act in the way he is teaching me here? *How* would I do that? *Where? Who* might help me?"

These are just sample questions to get you started. Starting with these six words, you can ask all sorts of things. It's like dancing: you probably had to learn and memorize some steps before you had the courage to get out on the dance floor. But once you started, the music took over and you just did what came naturally. It is like that when you meditate. Just start thinking, and the first thing you know, you and God will be one.

Responding is the most important step. Everything you do when you meditate is meant to lead you to *decisions*.

If you find that nothing comes to you when you are reflecting—if you ask all the questions and just come up blank—don't worry. Just go to step three. Ask yourself, "How can I *respond* to this? What could I *do*, what concrete choice could I make that would show I believe what I read here? How can I *put into action* what Jesus says here?"

You don't have to do anything impressive or even significant. A "token gesture" is enough, as long as it is an action, an act of *choice*. For example, you read Jesus' words, "Love one another as I have loved you." You get no great thoughts. So you ask, "What can I do, right now, to love someone else as Jesus loves me?"

Your first thought might be, "Die for them?" Scratch that. Not realistic. So you ask, "Well, how could I show love for somebody in some way, no matter how small?"

You can always find an answer if you think small enough. Suppose you decide just to smile at the next person who comes through the door? Or to say an Our Father for someone you aren't speaking to? Those are both real responses. Good responses. Just do one, and you have made a good meditation!

If you *read* what Jesus says, *reflect* on it (with or without getting any great thoughts), and *respond* in some concrete choice, you have "meditated," prayed over Scripture in a way that is real. You have let the word of God have a real influence on your life.

If it seems to be only a very tiny influence, don't worry. Remember that God is a negotiator. All he wants to do is get you to the table. If you keep sitting down with him, eventually he will talk you into doing everything he wants.

But if you don't make any decisions at all, meditation is useless. Jesus said:

> *Everyone who hears these words of mine and acts on them will be like a wise man who built his house on rock. The rain fell, the floods came, and the winds blew and beat on that house, but it did not fall, because it had been founded on rock.*
>
> *And everyone who hears these words of mine and does not act on them will be like a foolish man who built his house on sand. The rain fell, and the floods came, and the winds blew and beat against that house, and it fell—and great was its fall! (Matthew 7:24–27)*

That is the biggest mistake people make when they are reading the Bible or meditating: they don't decide on anything they will do about what they have read. It is just a "head trip." Head trips don't lead anywhere. If you don't make choices, you are just running laps inside your head and getting nowhere.

The same is true of preaching. What decision did you come to after the last homily you heard at Mass? What choice did it lead you to? If all it did was make you feel good, you were "building your house on sand." The first wind that came along blew those feelings right out of your heart. Feelings don't last. Choices do; especially *commitments.*

A free choice is a glorious, experienced moment of freedom. A commitment is a moment of freedom that endures. Meditation on the Bible should lead us to commitments. Commitments are the "structure" of our personalities. They determine who we are.

God creates us as *what* we are—human beings, men, women. But we create ourselves as the *who* our names stand for. When our names are finally written on our tombstones, they will mean whatever we have made them mean by all of our free choices, good and bad.

When we meditate, the goal is to let Jesus be an active partner with us as we go about the process of creating ourselves by choices. We let him give input. We hear what he thinks about things we are planning to do. Or about things we are doing without ever thinking about them. We learn from him new ways of seeing things that would never have occurred to us, new ways of doing things. When we drink with him, he serves us "new wine." It is exciting. Intoxicating. *But only if our goal is to do something.* There is nothing more useless than a thought we never act on.

Let's balance the picture a little. Sure, sometimes when we meditate (or, more precisely, "contemplate"), all we are doing is looking at the goodness of God, admiring what he says or does, praising or thanking him, realizing his love for us.

Reading the Bible is a conversation with God in which he mostly tells us about himself. God created us to "know him, love him, and serve him." But to serve him as we should, we first have to know him. And love him. So reading the Bible and meditating on it is something we do to *know* God better. And love him more. It is not all about making practical choices, decisions, or "resolutions."

Or is it?

Isn't love a free choice? Isn't it a very practical, concrete choice just to decide we will *believe* what Jesus says? That we will trust in him? We may not be deciding, here and now, on some physical action we will do. But we are deciding to *believe*, and that is what makes us able to do what we should do when the moment comes.

In the Book of Proverbs, God said:

My child, keep my words and store up my commandments within you…keep my teachings as the apple of your eye; bind them on your fingers, write them on the tablet of your heart. Say to wisdom, "You are my sister," and call insight your intimate friend. (Proverbs 7:1–4)

Through meditation we want to let God's words "abide" in us. As Jesus said, "If you abide in me, and my words abide in you, ask for whatever you wish, and it will be done for you" (John 15:7). If his words abide in us, we will eventually ask for nothing except "Thy will be done."

"This is the covenant that I will make with the house of Israel after those days," says the Lord: "I will put my laws in their minds, and write them on their hearts. And I will be their God, and they shall be my people." (Jeremiah 31:33)

To meditate is to let God write his words on our hearts, and then to express what is in our hearts in everything we do.

My suggestion: Take five, ten, fifteen minutes to use the "three R's" on some Scripture text and see what happens.

Let God talk to you. Let Jesus teach you.

NEVER ASK AGAIN

An authentic Christian life is one that *raises eyebrows.*

Does this sound farfetched? Daunting? Something out of your range or "above your pay scale"? Then it's time to take a look at our third "nut and bolt," our third step.

The third step you need to take in order to grow into the fullness of life is to *dedicate* yourself to making *constant changes* in your lifestyle. What you are really doing in this third step is accepting the *mission* of Jesus. Getting involved in it. Making it your mission. The bottom line of this "nut and bolt" is a simple choice: to *keep making changes* in the way you live.

This isn't just "change for the sake of change," although Blessed John Henry Newman said, "To live is to change, and to be perfect is to have changed often." It is change for a very specific purpose: to *bear witness* to Jesus Christ, and to his resurrection, by making his divine life visible in you in your words and actions, in your lifestyle. This means *living in such a way that what you say and do cannot be explained unless the risen Jesus is alive and acting in you.*

As Pope Paul VI defined it, to "bear witness" to the Good News means to "radiate faith in values that go beyond current values, and hope in something not seen, that one would not dare to imagine"

(Pope Paul VI, *Evangelization in the Modern World*, no. 21). This is the "wordless witness" of a lifestyle that "stirs up irresistible questions" in the hearts of those who see how you live. "Why are you like this? Why do you live like that? What or who is it that inspires you?"

This might sound challenging, but all you have to do is promise God you will *never ask again* whether something is right or wrong. Instead, you will ask, "*How does this bear witness to Jesus Christ?*"

How will what you are about to do bear witness to what Jesus taught? To his truth? To his values? To his presence in you, guiding and empowering you to "live on the level of God"? But you *don't promise to do* what bears witness to him. All you promise is to *ask*. This is very important.

Let's be real. We all know that none of us is good enough always to do what bears witness to Jesus. So don't promise it. Never promise what you can't do; it is discouraging. Pretty soon you will just forget all about it. When you are dealing with God, don't ask, "What *should* I do?" (ideal). Ask instead, "What *could* I do?" (realistic).

If you promise something you actually can do, and can do so easily that you will never have a reason not to, you will be able to keep that promise. Then every time you do what you promised, you will feel encouraged. You are succeeding. You are living up to your word. God is happy with you and you are happy with yourself. You are getting somewhere.

If all you promise is to *ask*, what does that cost you? "Well, I might feel guilty if I don't do what I know will bear witness to Jesus. It will make me conscious that I am not the kind of Christian I ought to be."

Forget guilt. We all have a long way to go. What we are talking about here is not perfection; it is *growth*. As Newman said, "To be perfect is to have *changed* often." He also said, "Nothing would be done at all if we waited until we could do it so well that no one could find fault with it." That is true of the Christian life. None of us lives it so well that no one could find fault with what we do. So the difference between the growing and the inert is simply *dedication to change*.

Jesus knows what not to expect of us. All he asks is *forward motion*. As we said above, God is a negotiator. He is so supremely confident of his ability to talk us into anything he wants, that all he asks at the beginning is the tiniest commitment to keep dealing with him. Promise to keep asking what bears witness to him, and the first thing you know, he will have you actually bearing witness to him in almost everything you do.

In practice, to get you to dedicate yourself to making *constant changes* in your lifestyle, all God asks is your promise to *keep asking* what bears witness to him. That is enough. The rest will take care of itself.

The Mystery of Empowerment

Underlying this simple practice is a deep mystery. It is the mystery of *empowerment to live on the level of God*. In early Christian preaching this was called "the gift of the Spirit."

When Peter announced the Good News, he called people to "Repent, and be baptized so that your sins may be forgiven; *and you will receive the gift of the Holy Spirit.*" If anyone did not receive the gift of the Spirit at baptism, the apostles knew something was missing, and did something about it (see Acts 8:14–17). Today we omit the last phrase. We just promise that baptism will "take away original sin" and give people "grace." We don't mention the "gift of the Holy Spirit." And if we did, most Catholics wouldn't know what we are talking about! But the gift of the Spirit is *power*, divine empowerment, the *mystical experience* of knowing you are being empowered to act on the level of God.

The gift of empowerment allows us to live out in action the divine life of God we received at baptism. We bear witness to the resurrection of Jesus by a lifestyle that cannot be explained without it. We live God's lifestyle, the lifestyle Jesus chose. Not in all its details, of course—we aren't going to be itinerant preachers living on alms—but in its basic, guiding principles. (You will find most of them in the Sermon on the Mount, in the Gospel of Matthew, chapters five to seven.)[11]

Jesus was God living as a human being, and a human being living on the level of God. This was visible in the way he spoke and acted. He, at least, claimed it was visible:

> *I have a testimony greater than John's. The works that the Father has given me to complete, the very works that I am doing, testify on my behalf that the Father has sent me.*
>
> *If I am not doing the works of my Father, then do not believe me. But if I do them, even though you do not believe me, believe the works, so that you may know and understand that the Father is in me and I am in the Father.*
>
> *Whoever has seen me has seen the Father...Do you not believe that I am in the Father and the Father is in me? The words that I say to you I do not speak on my own; but the Father who*

dwells in me does his works. Believe me that I am in the Father and the Father is in me; but if you do not, then believe me because of the works themselves. (John 5:36; 10:37–38; 14:9–11)

Obviously, Jesus thought no one could explain his life or his life-style without recognizing the life of God, the presence and power of the Father, in him. By "works" Jesus means much more than "miracles." He means everything he does to accomplish his purpose on earth.

For us who have "become Christ" by baptism, who share in his divine life and mission, all our "works" should express this new level of life in us and contribute to the new purpose it gives us. Nothing we do should be merely human in its beginning (motivation) or in its end (goal). It should not come from what is just human in us, or wind up being—or even appearing to be—a merely human act. Both the source and the summit of everything we do should be the power and glory of God: the glory of Jesus living in us, act-ing *with us, in us,* and *through us.* This, St. Paul said, was the whole of his preaching in a nutshell:

I became the servant of Christ's body, that is, the church, according to God's commission that was given to me for you, to make the word of God fully known, the mystery that has been hidden throughout the ages and generations but has now been revealed to his saints. [Through me] God chose to make known how great among the Gentiles are the riches of the glory of this mystery, which is Christ in you, the hope of glory (see Colossians 1:24–27).

Your mission as a Christian and as a prophet, anointed and

consecrated in baptism, is to make the word of God fully known by making this mystery—which is Christ in you—visible.

Christ in you: this is the source and summit of your Christian life. In you Christ is "growing to full stature," gradually bringing everything human in you into conformity with its divine counterpart in him: your thoughts into conformity with his thoughts; your desires into conformity with his desires; your way of acting as human into conformity with his way of acting as God. This is what your Christian life is all about. This is your present, seen in the light of your past and your future. You live to *grow* into the full realization, the full experience, and the full revelation of "this mystery, which is *Christ in you, the hope of glory.*"

This is the mystery and the glory of human life on earth. What is really happening is that Jesus is "growing to full stature" in every redeemed member of the human race. He is working in each one to bring about God's plan, "hidden throughout the ages and generations but now revealed to his holy ones." At the end of the world Jesus will stand forth in glory as one Body, head and members, all perfectly one "in the unity of the faith, and of the knowledge of the Son of God," all having become mature, grown up to "the measure of the stature which belongs to the fullness of Christ."

At the end, St. Augustine says, "There will be but one Christ, loving himself." And that is what the church is today: "one Christ, building himself up in love."

St. Paul proclaims this as the "work" of the church and of every member in it:

Speaking the truth in love [in deeds and lifestyle more than in

*words], we must grow up in every way into him who is the head,
into Christ, from whom the whole body, joined and knit together by
every ligament with which it is equipped, as each part is working
properly, promotes the body's growth in building itself up in love.
(Ephesians 4:15–16)*

A stagnant Christianity is a false Christianity. We were plunged
into the living waters of baptism to come alive! We show we are
alive, alive by the divine life of God, by Christ's life in us, when the
words and actions that make up our lifestyle cannot be explained
without it.

This is what it means to *bear witness* to Christ—to announce
the Good News, to be the visible sign and proof of his resurrection,
to make visible his risen life in us, to live out, and live up to, our
baptismal consecration and commitment as *prophets*.

The nuts and bolts of this is just to promise God you will *never
ask again* whether something is right or wrong. You will ask, before
every choice and decision, before you buy or sell, eat or drink, speak
or choose to remain silent, *"How does this bear witness to the values of
Jesus Christ?"*

Do that and you will live.

EVERYONE YOU MEET

The fourth nut and bolt you need in order to grow into the fullness of life is to *let Jesus express himself through you* to every person you deal with.

Yes, this is an ongoing mystical experience, and a very deep one, but it is not as "out of this world" as it may sound. In fact, it is very down to earth. And that is the key to it.

In this fourth step, Jesus Christ, the divine Word of God, "takes flesh" by expressing his divine truth and love to others in and through your human, physical words and actions. You are his body. When Jesus expresses the divine truth of God through you, in human words formed by your human lips and "sent forth" by your human breath passing through your physical vocal cords, the Word of God is being made flesh in you, for others.

This is the key mystery of Christianity: the Word made flesh in Jesus Christ—and in us who are his body today. We have seen that this is the mystery that contains and sums up all of Paul's preaching: "this mystery, which is *Christ in you, the hope of glory.*" Christ made flesh in you. Christ speaking and acting in you as in his own body, making audible and visible the glory of God. The mystery that you have *become Christ.*

Just Express It

Let's get down to the nuts and bolts of making this mystery part of your daily life and experience. You do that by putting the mystery into practice.

How do you do this? You do it by deciding that, in every encounter with another person, you will make sure that everything you say and do is an *expression of your faith*. Or of the *hope* you have that is based on faith. Or of the *love* in your heart that is God's own divine love for the person you are dealing with. That is not as abstract as it sounds.

Let's say you are going through the checkout line at Walmart. The woman at the cash register says, "Fifteen dollars." You pay her fifteen dollars and walk out. You have just denied the faith! How? Not explicitly, of course, but implicitly, *by ignoring it*, by acting as if what you believe by faith does not mean anything to you; as if it were not true.

Suppose the woman behind the counter is your blood sister. If you treat her like that, won't you be hearing from her as soon as she gets off from work? "What is the matter with you? You went through my checkout line today and treated me as if you didn't even know me! Hey, I'm your sister, you know. You didn't ask me how I felt. You didn't say anything about my hairdo. You didn't mention it is raining outside or tell me to drive carefully on the way home. You spoke to me as if I were nothing but an employee behind the counter. A functionary. Didn't you happen to notice that I am your *sister*? What is the matter with you?"

The truth is that every woman behind that counter is your sister. Anyone who has received the divine life of God that makes us all children of the Father is our brother or sister in Christ. To ignore that, to act as if this truth of faith did not exist, is implicitly to deny the faith. We express ourselves as much by what we don't say as by what we do say.

So to let Jesus Christ express his divine truth *"with you, in you, and through you,"* you need to deal with every person you meet in a way that expresses, embodies, makes visible in words and actions, the invisible truth that is in your heart by *faith.* That is *ministry.*

How do you do that? Simple. Without saying anything explicit, you simply deal with each person as you would with your blood sister or brother. You find a way, even if it is through meaningless small talk, to make it clear that you see the person as more than just a functionary—as a person, a human being like yourself, with the same needs, feelings, and dignity.

If you say, for example, "Hey, you're lucky to be working inside; it's raining out there," you aren't really saying anything except— without actually saying the words—"I see you as a person like myself, not just as an employee doing a job." *That* is how you express in and through words the faith-vision in your heart.

The truth is—and as time goes on you will become more and more aware of it, quietly, in the back of your mind—it is not just you expressing your faith. It is *Jesus in you* expressing the truth he sees, expressing his divine vision in and through your words, letting himself as the divine Word of God be "made flesh" in your human words and actions.

That makes every encounter with others both *ministry* and a *mystical experience!* An experience of interaction with God through *surrender* to what Jesus in you wishes to express through your human body, which is his body. An experience of *union* with Jesus in action. A mystical experience.

The same is true every time you treat people with the kind of love you know Jesus in your heart has for them. You don't have to explain what you are doing or why. Just do it. That lets Jesus express his love *with* you, *in* you, and *through* you—to give life, to increase the divine life of God in others by communicating to them, in and through your physical words and actions, his divine truth, his divine love.

When he does this in you and through you, you experience the fulfillment of his *promise*:

> *I am the vine, you are the branches. Those who abide in me and I in*
> *them bear much fruit, because apart from me you can do nothing...*
> *You did not choose me but I chose you. And I appointed you to go*
> *and bear fruit, fruit that will last. (John 15:5–16)*

You hear the angel saying to you the words spoken to Mary: "Blessed is the fruit..." not "of your womb," but "of your life." Then you can say with Jesus, to everyone you meet, "*This is my body, given for you.*" Just by surrendering your body to Jesus to be the instrument, the medium of his self-expression, you mediate his divine life to others. You give your "flesh for the life of the world."

The experience of doing this grows on you. It becomes a clearer and clearer mystical experience of acting in *union* with Jesus. All you have to do is make a habit of *expressing* your divine faith, your divine hope, your divine love in and through every human interaction with others. This was Paul's exhortation to the baptized: "present your [physical] bodies as a living sacrifice...which is your spiritual service" (Romans 12:1).

Is that simple and clear enough to work with? Concrete enough to be a "nut and bolt"?

Let's make it even more concrete. What one, specific, even more concrete practice can you adopt that will "spark" this, keep you expressing faith, hope, and love through all your interactions with others? What is the nut that will fit your particular bolt?

What works for me is something I learned from a rancher in Texas who was also a stockbroker. I had brought a bunch of college students to help with a high school retreat near him. We were staying at his ranch and playing football with his kids when one of the college girls came up to me and asked: "What is going on here? They haven't had a fight. They haven't even argued. They throw the ball to the little kids and let them catch it. What's with these people? In my family we'd have killed each other by now!"

I said, "Let's ask." So we asked my friend's wife, "What is the secret of this family?"

She hooked her thumb toward her husband and said, "Him."

"What do you mean, 'him'? What does he do?"

She said, "It's very simple. *Everything good he sees in anybody, he tells them.* That's it."

I had known that man most of my life and never noticed what he was doing, it was so natural. So now I began to watch.

His daughter walked through the room. He said, "You look good in that dress." His son brought his plate back to the kitchen after supper. He said, "That was a nice thing to do for your mother." The most natural thing in the world. But how many do it? I decided to imitate him. It changed my life.

When I went back to my parish, I began telling people the good things I noticed in them. Then one Sunday a few weeks later, I was in the presider's chair at Mass, looking out at the congregation. I noticed I was feeling very happy. I asked myself why.

"It's because these are such good people," I told myself. "I'm just glad to be here with them."

But I didn't feel that way a few weeks ago. What changed?

Then I realized what had happened. When I began to *tell* people what was good in them, I began to *notice* what was good in them.

A basic principle of life: "What you praise you will appreciate. What you do not praise you will not appreciate." Fundamental and life-transforming. As pastor it transformed me from manager into minister. Then I extended the practice.

Now, if I go into the bathroom at the airport and someone is mopping the floor, I say, "Hey, the floor looks great. Thank you for keeping this place so clean." (One janitor looked at me dumb-founded: "No one has ever said that to me before!")

Think about that. If you came home from work and found your husband, wife, or one of your kids mopping the floor, wouldn't you say something? So why don't we thank the people who are paid to do it? Why don't we thank everybody for everything? Jesus would. It makes us family.

I have often "pushed the envelope" on this, complimenting per-fect strangers on their dress, their smile, their children, the work they are doing. If I see a couple carrying a baby I say, "Congratulations! And in the name of the human race, thank you!" No one has ever gotten mad.

I live in a neighborhood where there is racial tension. When I cross the street in front of my house and a car is passing by, I wave. I often feel like an idiot, but I wave. I would if my brother were in the car. Most wave back. One man, whom I've never met, will honk at me first now, laughing and waving hello. It changes the neighborhood.

So here is a very specific nut that just might fit your bolt: *Form the habit of telling everyone you meet whatever you see in them that is good.* You will experience Christ loving in you. *Own* the experience. Acknowledge it. Let Jesus express his truth, his love, to every person you deal with—all day, every day. This is what it means to live out— and live up to—your baptismal anointing as priest.

Priest and Victim

We could stop here. But let's go one level deeper into the mystery of ministry.

To minister as a "priest in the Priest" is also to become a "victim in the Victim." You let Jesus *offer himself* to others in you by letting him give physical expression to his divine truth and love through your bodily words and actions. He offers himself for others *with you, in you, and through you.* You offer yourself for others *"through him, with him, and in him"*—your "flesh for the life of the world."

The Victim that Jesus offers as Priest on the cross is himself, his own body. You, as a member of his body, having "become Christ" by baptism, offer that sacrifice *with him, in him,* and *through him* as a sharer in his priesthood. But since the Victim that Jesus offers is his own body, and you are his body, if you are doing the offering with him as priest in the Priest, you are also offering yourself with him as victim in the Victim.

In Jesus, Priest and Victim are the same. Jesus gave life to the world by dying. We give life as priests in the Priest by dying to ourselves.

Self-Revelation Is Vulnerability

How do we "die to ourselves" as "victims"? By *self-expression*.

To express oneself is to reveal oneself. To reveal oneself is to be vulnerable. And we are scared to death of this. We are afraid to express our opinions, especially our religious opinions. We are even more afraid to express our emotions, above all our religious emotions. Look at the teenagers at Mass. They make a point of looking indifferent. To be involved is not cool. In them we adults see ourselves without the disguise of token participation.

We might express some enthusiasm at a football game, but never in church! Football is something to jump up and down and scream about. But not religion. When we are celebrating the redemption of the world at Mass we make it very clear there is nothing to be excited about. Many people won't even sing. Those who do may sing with their lips, but not with their hearts.

Why? Because we are scared to death to put any life into our celebration of religion, scared to have anyone see us showing felt devotion to God! We are afraid to look "holy." Or "fervent." Or even enthusiastic. If we revealed ourselves like this, we would feel we were dying.

And we would be. We would be dying to self. Dying to self to give life to others. Putting our fears to death to make the Mass come alive. We would all be *ministering* to each other as *priests* through that "full, conscious, active participation" the bishops tried to bring about by reforming the liturgy at the Second Vatican Council.

The Mystery of the Cross

By dying to ourselves we could give life to the world. We could make the Mass life-giving for others instead of a drag. We might even keep the youth from dropping out! But we won't. We refuse to be "victims in the Victim." We won't even accept to be "priests in the Priest." We prefer not to be "ministers in the pews." We don't accept to "offer ourselves" to others at Mass in the "ministry of self-expression." Self-expression costs too much.

To really *express* ourselves—to express the faith, the hope, the love we celebrate at Mass—we would have to *expose* ourselves. Die to our fears. Drop our reserves. Shed our inhibitions. Give up control. Be spontaneous. It is just too much to ask. We refuse to do it. We want Jesus to offer himself on the cross for us, but we don't want to offer ourselves with him. His "flesh for the life of the world," but not ours. We are just afraid.

If we admit this, we can go to another level. We can confront the "mystery of the cross"—the deepest challenge of Christian life—as it touches us, becomes real in our daily lives, becomes a matter of personal choice.

Jesus said, "Whoever does not carry the cross and follow me cannot be my disciple" (Luke 14:27). Did you ever think "carrying the cross" might mean a practical challenge like forcing yourself to sit up front at Mass? And sing? Enthusiastically? Or to share your deepest religious experiences with your spouse or children or a friend: how you *feel* about God, what Jesus Christ really means to you, how you think he has acted in your life? Or to get into a discussion group? To tell a stranger hello? To smile at the cleaning lady? To show more than polite respect for everyone? Would any of the above feel to you like dying?

That is the cost of ministry. It is the same price Jesus paid, who was crucified because he expressed himself, and who on the cross went on to give the most passionate expression of love ever given. Are you willing to strip yourself of your shielding reserves and join him? Are you willing to take up the cross of self-expression? Self-revelation? Self-exposure?

We simply don't *experience* what is inside of us until we *express* it. If we "keep our light under a bushel basket," we not only fail to "give light to all in the house"; we remain in the dark ourselves.

It is a law of physics that we don't see any objects except when they *reflect* light. In outer space, astronauts facing away from the sun see nothing but utter, total darkness. The light of the sun itself is not visible unless it is reflected back from some physical object.

It is a law of the spiritual life that, unless we are looking directly at God and his truth, the light of faith itself in our hearts is darkness to us unless we see it reflected back from realities on which we shine it.

We sing, "*This little light of mine, I'm gonna let it shine....*" Why? Because if I don't, I won't even know I have it! The same is true of love. I don't know I love until I experience myself loving somebody. And I don't experience that until I *give* love, let it go out from me, *express* it in words and actions.

St. John of the Cross said, "Where you don't find love, put love and you will find it." When you don't experience love at Mass, express love and you will find it.

If you don't experience passion, get passionate in your self-expression and you will experience it. But if you won't "lose yourself" in full and free expression of what is in you, you will never "find yourself" as a person who loves God. And you won't *give* light or love to others in a life-giving way. At Mass you will be dead yourself and deadening to others.

Many—perhaps most—Catholics right now don't experience the light or love that is in them by grace because they don't express it. But they don't *feel* they are holding back, because they don't let themselves feel anything at all. They have such a tight hold on their emotions that their emotions are not even fighting back.

That is why our churches are empty. Even the full ones are empty if we look at who should be there. As a church, Americans are barely able to reproduce themselves. We are not a reproductive community of life, just a self-perpetuating culture of inertia. At least, it often appears that way.

Now I know that appearances are deceptive. I just got carried away. The church is really alive and vigorous—if not in some places, then in others. God promised, "I will pour out my Spirit upon all flesh. Your sons and your daughters shall prophesy, your young men shall see visions, and your old men shall dream dreams" (Joel 2:28; Acts 2:17). This is happening—and it's happening now. Sometimes we see it. And when we don't, we wait for it with hope.

This hope "does not disappoint us, because God's love has been poured into our hearts through the Holy Spirit that has been given to us" (Romans 5:5). Jesus is risen. The Spirit is given. Regardless of what we see at the present moment, we look forward to the "end time." We "await the blessed hope and the manifestation of the glory of our great God and Savior, Jesus Christ" (Titus 2:13).

In the meantime, we work to make that happen. And that brings us to the "nuts and bolts" of our fifth step toward the "perfection of love." This is the phase of total *abandonment* to the work of transforming the world as a sharer in Christ's *kingship*.

What Steps Have You Taken So Far?

Your first step was to cultivate ongoing *awareness* of the new identity you received at baptism, when you "became Christ." For this you *use the WIT prayer*.

Your second step was to *commit* yourself to be a *disciple* of the mind and heart of God. As a sign and start of this, you *put a Bible on your pillow*.

Your third step was to dedicate yourself to the *mission* of proclaiming the Good News as a *prophet*. For this you promised to *ask the question* before everything you do: *"How does this bear witness to Christ?"*

Your fourth step was to *surrender* to your *ministry* as *priest* by letting Jesus *express* himself through all your words and actions. To do this, you consciously express your faith, hope, and love in every act of dealing with people. Concretely, you might begin just by *telling people what you see in them that is good*.

Now to step five!

JUST NOTICE

The fifth nut and bolt you need to put together in order to grow into the fullness of life is simply to start *noticing*, wherever you are, anything that needs to be changed.

People notice things they feel *responsible* for. To make a point of noticing everything around you that calls for change is to acknowledge—and experience—responsibility for God's world. For everything Jesus came to redeem. That is, for everything. Yes, this too is a mystical experience!

This responsibility is yours because at baptism you were consecrated as *king*, that is, as a sharer, a partner, in Christ's mission of reforming and ruling over every area and activity of human life on earth. In addition to being a *prophet* and *priest*, you are an anointed "*steward of the kingship of Christ.*" This is an element of the mystery of your life. To be conscious of it is to be having a mystical experience.

Because God anointed you to do it, you are committed by baptism to *work for change*. But on the level of nuts-and-bolts spirituality, your first step into living out this commitment is just to form the habit of *noticing*.

Just by noticing, you will be experiencing an initial acceptance of *responsibility* for establishing the reign of God over everything you can influence. God will take it farther. All you have to do is begin.

There used to be a saying: "If you're not confused, you don't understand the situation." Today—and every day—we could change that to: "If you're not distressed...." Or, "If you're not angry...." There is so much wrong in our world, so much deceit, so much injustice, so much wrong thinking and deliberate distortion of truth—in the church as well as in family and social life, business, and politics—that our natural reaction is "fight or flight." If we have any idea of what is going on, it makes us feel like putting our fist in someone's face or putting our head in the sand. Most people do a little of both. Jesus did neither. And we are called to respond as Jesus did; because in baptism we *became Christ.*

We were anointed, solemnly consecrated by God himself, to continue Christ's "messianic mission" as *prophet, priest,* and *king.* To do that is our "job description" as Christians. And the last one is the most difficult. It could get us killed.

We might get away with bearing prophetic witness by a lifestyle so inspired by the gospel that it raises eyebrows. And we won't be hurt too much if we accept the vulnerability of "dying"—dying to our self-enclosed defensiveness—when we "offer our bodies as a living sacrifice" to God and others through *self-expression,* giving physical expression to Christ's truth, Christ's love within us as "priests in the Priest," in order to give life to others—our "flesh for the life of the world."

But when we start making *changes* in the world—from little changes in our family life to taking on the transformation of society—people get mad. What we do in our own lives they may accept as our business. But when we start changing the world others live in, the culture they are comfortable with, the customs they take for granted, we stir up a hornet's nest. If we start rocking the boat, they may just throw us out of it. That is what they did to Jesus.

The Pharisees portrayed in the Gospels hated Jesus because as *Prophet* he spoke truth. And the love he showed for others as *Priest* made them look bad as he "went about all the cities and villages, teaching in their synagogues, and proclaiming the good news of the kingdom, and curing every disease and every sickness" (Matthew 4:23; 9:35). But they crucified him for claiming to be *King*.

Those who had power in the People of God that was the "church" at that time—the "chief priests," scribes, and Pharisees—were the ones who plotted and brought about Jesus' death. And their motive was clear:

> *The chief priests and the Pharisees called a meeting of the council, and said, "What are we to do? This man is performing many signs. If we let him go on like this, everyone will believe in him, and the Romans will come and destroy both our holy place and our nation." (John 11:47–48)*

What they were defending was the *status quo* of society and their position in it. The accusation they made against Jesus to Pilate was: "We found this man perverting our nation, forbidding us to pay taxes to the emperor, and saying that he himself is the Messiah, a king." This was the charge on the inscription Pilate put on the cross. It read, "Jesus of Nazareth, the King of the Jews" (Luke 23:2; John 19:19).

Things are still the same. Anyone who threatens the position or power of another—in church or state, in family life, in social circles, or in the corporate structures of business—is going to pay for it. That means anyone who works for *change*. And that is precisely what we are consecrated and committed to do as *stewards* of Christ's kingship.

But we don't have to jump into it all at once. God's way is to start small. He inspires us to do easy things first, things that don't cost anything, like just *noticing* what is not completely right around us.

God knows that if we notice, we will eventually react. When we see something that is wrong, the Holy Spirit in our hearts will inspire us little by little to take action—just little actions at first, like picking up a piece of paper off the floor, even though it is someone else's "job." As *stewards* of the kingship of Christ, we begin to see everything as our job.

This is what managers do. A restaurant manager would pick up a napkin off the floor without waiting for someone else to do it. The manager is responsible for everything. And as stewards of Christ's kingship, we are responsible for everything in his kingdom.

We can't *do* everything, of course. No manager can. But if we have a sense of *responsibility* for everything, we will notice everything, and then do what we can do. We will make responsible decisions not to get involved in what we haven't the time or talent for, or in what conflicts with other responsibilities.

We can't *do* everything. But we can *notice* everything. That is the first step—to start noticing is the nuts-and-bolts decision that makes our baptismal consecration as stewards of the kingship of Christ real, authentic. When we start noticing, we realize we have accepted *responsibility*.

To "realize" means two things: it is both to "discover" and to "make real." When we commit ourselves to start *noticing* everything around us that calls for change, we "discover" or *experience* ourselves as responsible stewards of Christ's kingship. And we make our consecration to that real in our lives.

That is the nuts and bolts of step five. Just start *noticing*.

We could stop here. And you can stop reading now, if you want. But if you care to look ahead and prepare for the challenges you will face as you take responsibility for changing the world, read on.

See, Judge, Act

The guiding formula for the Catholic Action movement after the upheaval of the Second World War was "See, judge, act." The Young Christian Students or Young Christian Workers would meet in small groups. Each would bring up some problem noticed in school or at work ("see"). Then the group would discuss the solution ("judge"). Finally, individuals or the group as a whole would make a decision about what to do ("act"). Out of this process the Cursillo Movement was born.[12]

You may have noticed that this formula is the same, in different words, as the "three R's" of the Nuts and Bolts of Meditation we discussed earlier. To "see, judge, act" is really communal meditation. It is a way of "remembering, reflecting, and responding" as a group—with the "common union" of a *community*.

The Need for Community

You can't do this alone. You will need the support of the Christian community in order to live this fifth step in its fullness—which will take you far beyond the nuts and bolts of just *noticing*. That is why we have the church.

We have to be honest. The truth, the reality of Catholic life today, is that many people do not "experience community" in their parishes—at least, not that "communion in the Holy Spirit," that mystical experience that we wish for each other at Mass.

What we call "Christian community" is not just a "common unity" of doctrine, morals, and cultural practices. Professing the same truths and keeping the same rules can unite people strongly to each other and violently against others, but it is not Christian community.

Many Catholics who don't know much about their faith or care very much about its laws still find themselves emotionally attached to the church through the "practices" they grew up with, like receiving ashes on Ash Wednesday and palms on Palm Sunday. They might attend Mass on Christmas and Easter and have their children baptized, even confirmed. But this is not "religious unity." It is token adherence to "cultural Catholicism."

Another form of cultural Catholicism—on a deeper but perhaps more dangerous level because it so easily disguises itself as authentic faith—is the "common unity" of those who sincerely profess the doctrines taught in church, without bothering to really understand them. These people keep the rules—on the level of good, ethical behavior that all decent people accept—but they have no inkling of what it means to live on the divine level of the life of God that they received at baptism. Their lifestyle does not bear witness to the values of Jesus. They are just "nice people," good by the standards of their peer group.

They "go" to Mass. They may even sing—politely, according to the rules—but the Mass is not a mystical experience for them, and their lack of enthusiasm can keep it from being a mystical experience for many others. There can be no "communion in the

Holy Spirit" between people whose "common union"—conscious, at least—is just a common human acceptance of the same doctrinal words, moral laws, and external devotional practices. Even on those occasions when the beauty of the ceremonies and music, or the inspirational words of the homily, stir their hearts, they are still not experiencing the mystery of the Mass. And they do not experience "communion in the Holy Spirit" with those who do.

What Is "Communion in the Holy Spirit"?

It is the experience, consciously recognized by all, of being alive with the *life of God*. It is the awareness of *divine enlightenment*. It is the discernment of *divine empowerment* present in oneself and others whose life and words and actions cannot be explained without it. It is the experience of Jesus Christ expressing himself in and through the physical words, body language, and behavior of those who are manifestly his body on earth. It is the shared, inexplicable *hope* in the coming of the kingdom that Christians sustain in each other by working together to bring it about—especially when there is no human prospect of success and the advocates of change are being persecuted, ostracized, even murdered. The ultimate "communion in the Holy Spirit" is that of the martyrs, who abandon themselves and all they have to the work of the kingdom, choosing to lose life in order to find it for themselves and others.

We Are All Called to Leadership

When our responsibility leads us to notice, and our noticing leads us to perceive what needs to be done and how to do it, we are called to exercise *leadership*.

Leadership is just stewardship in action. Very few people have the *authority* that empowers them to get things done by others. But *leadership* is not the same as authority and does not require it, any more than authority automatically makes one a leader. People obey authorities out of commitment; but they follow leaders voluntarily, whenever they believe that someone knows the way to go. So anyone who happens to see what needs to be done in a particular situation is by that very fact called to exercise leadership and is consecrated by baptism to do so as a *steward* of the kingship of Christ.

We have a chance to practice leadership weekly, at every Sunday Mass. If we rise to the challenge and do it, there is hope we will grow into exercising leadership everywhere we are.

This is what we should all be conscious of when we gather together for Mass! Here is a weekly, ground-level challenge: as *stewards* of the kingship of Christ, we are responsible for *making Mass the experience it should be*, for ourselves and others.

Jesus said, "When I am *lifted up* from the earth, I will draw all people to myself" (John 12:32). Is it really too farfetched to hope that if we really "lift up our hearts" at Mass, and lift up our voices, and lose ourselves in lifting up praise and prayer to God, we will "draw all people" to the church?

Why aren't they coming now? Because the Mass is dead. Or only half alive. (Okay, maybe as many as three-quarters of the people in your parish sing; how many raise the rafters?) And why is the Mass dead? Because the people are. What do I mean? The people are dead, because, paradoxically—they refuse to die to themselves. They are afraid to "lose their life" by losing themselves in the crowd. By joining in. By expressing without reserve the love that is in their hearts, the light that is within them. If they did, they would "find their life" in the act of "losing themselves" by expressing it.

If we consciously *notice* what is missing at Sunday Mass, this presents us with a weekly challenge and opportunity. We can ask ourselves, "What can I do about it?" When we see something—and God will make sure we will—we have the chance and the choice to exercise leadership.

The liturgy will be reformed, and the Mass will come alive, not through what the presiding priest does at the altar, but through the level of participation given by the "priests in the pews."

What the Mass is and becomes, for you and for your children, for the rest of the people in the pews and for those who no longer fill them, depends, more than on anything else, on how the *congregation* expresses itself.

So let's take a look now at the nuts and bolts of your own participation at Mass.

The "WEEKLY CRISIS" *of* EUCHARIST

The church calls the Mass the source and summit of the Christian life. Why? Because this is where we *experience*—and this is what *nourishes* the experience of—"the glory *of this mystery*, which is *Christ in you, the hope of glory*" (Colossians 1:27).

Obviously, what we "get out of Mass" depends on what we bring to it, and on what others bring to it, because the Mass must be a communal experience to be "real."

Do you want to get into the nuts and bolts of daily spirituality? It is simple. Go to Mass. And *notice* what you see.

We are back where we started: *noticing* what is missing in the Mass—which means what is missing in the Christian community—and being challenged, called, committed by our baptismal consecration as *stewards of Christ the King*, to do something about it.

What do we mean by "crisis"? A turning point, a time of decision that takes us up or down, makes us better or worse, draws us forward into the church's life or leaves us farther behind. So, every Eucharist is, or should be, a moment of crisis.

The Mass is a challenge no one escapes. Every week it summons us. Every week our choices take us up or take us down; they bring us more deeply into the Mass or make our experience more shallow. We either go or we don't. If we go, we either participate "fully, actively, consciously" or we don't. What we decide to do will help create or destroy the experience of Eucharist for ourselves and others, help increase or help diminish "communion in the Holy Spirit." The way we participate will bring us closer to God and others or make us more distant from both. There is no other way. The Mass is there. Every week it calls us into crisis. We have to choose. And our choices determine who we are.

So rise to the challenge. Exult in it. Greet it with joy. Find excitement in meeting the waves at Mass. Dive into it. Bring your anger, your sadness, your confusion into church with you. Insist on going out with love, joy, and peace. Go for it! It's "crisis time"!

The Nuts and Bolts of Participating at Mass

The key to full, conscious, active participation in Eucharist is very simple: *pay attention*. Do this, and you will never be bored at Mass.

Listen to the words. Hear what they are saying. Ask yourself whether you understand them. If not, pursue their meaning until you do.

In the responses—the words you are called to say out loud—listen to what you are saying. Ask if you mean what the words say. Try to say them as if you mean them. When you can't, accept the challenge to grow. The Mass won't let you stagnate.

For example, in the Introductory Rites hear yourself—and the assembly—being introduced. See if you can consciously embrace the *new identity* that is being proclaimed.

In the Greeting, you hear the community identified as those who share in the *"grace of the Lord Jesus Christ."* Divine life. Everyone present is divine. Does that speak to you? The Greeting takes for granted all have experienced the *"love of the Father."* We share this common experience. We believe that we know what it is to be loved by God. (Or, if we don't, the Greeting gives us something to think about, a direction to pursue.)

Our "being together" is proclaimed as *"communion in the Holy Spirit."* It is an experience of mystical union with each other and God. If we do not experience it as that, we need to ask why not and how we can grow into it.

The Mass calls us to take seriously and absorb the mystery of who we are: the "breadth and length and height and depth" of what our life can be on this earth if we enter into it.

In the Penitential Act we make it clear that we all come together as equals. At Mass the only identity we claim besides our mystical union with God is our common condition as sinners. *"I confess to almighty God and to you, my brothers and sisters, that I have sinned."* We introduce ourselves as people who sin "in our thoughts, in our words, in what we have done and failed to do." There are no exceptions. Everyone present, whether pope, president, or prostitute, claims right of entry into the assembly under two titles only: son or daughter of God, and sinner. No other titles count. The community admits to the eucharistic celebration "all and only" those who introduce themselves as undifferentiated, equal children of the Father who are accepted and accept others as sinners. We leave all other identity at the door. If that is not made visible at Mass, if all do not feel equally accepted, you need to ask what you can do about it.

When we say, *"Lord, have mercy,"* we are entering into another mystery: our right to be heard as *family*. To "have mercy" means to "come to the aid of another out of a sense of *relationship.*" The Hebrew root from which "mercy" comes is the word for "womb." The Latin *pietas,* "piety" (in Spanish "have mercy" is *ten piedad*), is the virtue of family loyalty: the "gut bond" of relationship between parents and children, brothers and sisters. When we say, "Have mercy," we are praying as children of the Father. We pray to Jesus as his brothers and sisters. And more: we pray out of the sense of *identification* we have with Jesus as his own body. "In Christ" we pray as Christ praying to himself. Understand this. Hear it in the words of the *Kyrie.* Enter into it.

In the *Gloria,* join in hearing or singing the words as you would join others in reciting the pledge of allegiance in a moment of communal patriotic fervor. The *Gloria* proclaims what we stand for as a united community—not only what we believe in, but what we are committed to.

As a community, we are committed to *praise and thanksgiving*: "We *praise you, we bless you, we adore you, we give you thanks* for your great glory!" We are the people who do that. That is who we are. That is who you are. Make the words your own. Proclaim them from your heart.

Notice the progression into intimacy: "Lord *God,* heavenly *King,* almighty God and *Father!*" We are the community who knows God, not just as all-powerful Creator, but as *King* involved in our history on earth. And as *Father* sharing his own divine life with us.

We are the people who acknowledge Jesus, not just as "Lord God," but as "*Lamb of God who takes away the sins of the world.*" He is our *Savior.* He is "seated at the right hand of the Father." He will "receive our prayer." He will "have mercy on us."

If we *listen* during the Introductory Rites we will be challenged to know ourselves—to question, to ponder, to grow. This will enrich the identity we enter into and experience when we say the WIT prayer. And saying the WIT prayer will enrich the identity we experience at Mass.

Listen as a Disciple

The nuts and bolts of participation in the Liturgy of the Word are to listen to the readings as a *disciple*—that is, as a student bent on *learning*. Don't just sit back in the pew like someone in an audience, waiting for something to "hit you." If you do that, probably nothing will. The Scriptures were not written to be heard by an audience, or just to be read by individuals. They were written to be *recognized* with active faith as the *living words* of God, of God present and personally speaking his words, revealing his mind and heart to those who want to know him. They were written for people who listen prayerfully to learn—that is, for *students*, for "disciples," for those who *seek life* through *encountering God*.

For disciples, hearing or reading Scripture is prayer, a two-way conversation, the give and take of dialogue. It involves simultaneous activity, the ongoing, mutual revelation and response of two or more living persons who are interacting with each other in order to grow into one.

It is church teaching that there is a "real presence" of God in the scriptural words read at Mass. The bishops at Vatican II declared: "In the sacred books, the Father who is in heaven meets his children with great love and speaks with them…" (*On Divine Revelation*, no. 21).

The *General Instruction on the Roman Missal* repeats the same

Catholic belief: "When the Sacred Scriptures are read in the Church, *God himself speaks* to his people, and Christ, *present in his own word*, proclaims the Gospel" (no. 29).

So during the Liturgy of the Word at Mass, don't listen to "words" being read from a book. Be conscious of God speaking to you. Here. Now. Personally. And reply by *reflecting* on what you hear and *responding* to it in decisions. Listen with your ears, reflect with your mind, and respond with your heart. Be a whole person. And you will experience *enlightenment* by God.

If you have "put the Bible on your pillow," you will find that what you hear during Mass is becoming increasingly familiar to you. Listening to the readings will be like picking up a conversation where you left off.

"Go with the Flow"

Don't just listen. *Watch* the actions of the liturgy. Appreciate the symbolism. Be aware of what the movements, the gestures, are saying. Let them reveal to you what you are expressing, what you are called to be saying in your heart. Enter into the movements. Get into the action. "Go with the flow."

For example, during the Presentation of Gifts, almost everything is said before the presider speaks any words at all. The "gifts"—the bread and wine that will be offered as Christ's Body and Blood during the Eucharistic Prayer—are brought up from the back of the church, by lay members of the assembly passing through the whole congregation, to be placed on the altar. And on the plate there are, or should be, according to the *General Instruction of the Roman Missal* (no. 85), the same number of hosts as there are people present in the assembly.

All this is visible in the procession that comes forward to "present the gifts" of bread and wine. As you watch, you should ask, about everything you see, "Why?" Why are the gifts brought up from the back of the church? Why by laypersons? Why are they put on the altar? Why the same number of hosts as people present?

What you see is saying to you that, symbolically, the *whole congregation* is coming forward to place themselves on the altar. All present are "presenting their bodies as a living sacrifice," as they did at baptism, to be offered *with* Christ and *in* Christ during the Eucharistic Prayer.

This is, and should be for every individual present, a moment of intense recommitment. This is a time for you to say again what you said, or your parents and godparents said for you, at baptism: *I give you my body. I place myself on the altar to die with Christ, to rise as Christ, to live as his body on earth.*

Paul was speaking of baptism when he wrote: "I appeal to you, brothers and sisters...to *present your bodies as a living sacrifice*, holy and acceptable to God..." (Romans 12:1). At baptism you gave your body to become Christ's body, so that he might continue to live and carry out his mission in you, speaking and acting in your flesh. Now you reaffirm that gift, consciously, personally, as you are today—as all you have become and are at this moment in your life. You "present your body" to be Christ's body. And you dedicate yourself, as "mature in Christ," to continue his *mission* on earth.

To do this, you pledge to make your lifestyle bear *witness* to the divine life of God in you, to be different from the culture in a way that "stirs up irresistible questions" in the hearts of those who see how you live.

It is so you might bear witness to Christ as a *prophet* that Paul continues: "*Do not be conformed to this world*, but be *transformed* by the renewing of your mind, so that you may discern what is the will of God—what is *good and acceptable and perfect*" (Romans 12:2).

This is a summons to *continual conversion*, which in ground-level English means "a life of constant change." The bread and wine are put on the altar to be changed. By putting ourselves on the altar with them, we pledge to make *constant changes in our lifestyle*, until all that we do is not only "good," as free from sin, but "acceptable," as bearing witness to the truth and values taught by Jesus Christ, and even "perfect," as being the self-expression of Jesus himself speaking and acting through us.

The Presentation of Gifts invites us to reaffirm our dedication to the mission of bearing *prophetic witness*. On the nuts-and-bolts level of daily life, this means we pledge *never to ask again* just whether something is right or wrong, but to ask instead: "*How does this bear witness to the values of Christ?*" Entering consciously into the Presentation of Gifts feeds this pledge and is fed by it.

"My Body...Given to Everyone"

Next we move into the Eucharistic Prayer, which the *General Instruction of the Roman Missal* calls " the center and summit of the entire celebration." In this prayer the presider "unites the congregation with himself in the prayer that he addresses in the name of the entire community to God the Father through Jesus Christ in the Holy Spirit" (no. 78).

The point is, this is the *congregation's* prayer—really, the prayer of the whole church throughout the world. The priest at the altar is simply saying out loud the prayer that all the "priests in the pews"—all consecrated by baptism as "priests in the Priest"—are saying in their hearts. It is the prayer of the whole community, not just of the ordained priest, and all should be hearing and speaking the words with him in the deep silence and attention of their hearts.

"The meaning of the Prayer is that the *entire congregation* of the faithful should *join itself with Christ* in confessing the great deeds of God and in the offering of Sacrifice" (*General Instruction on the Roman Missal*, no. 78). What takes place at the altar is not because of the prayer or power of the ordained priest; it is God's response to the prayer of everyone there, who represent the whole church throughout the world. The *Instruction* is clear about this: the bread and wine become the Body and Blood of Christ because "*the Church implores* the power of the Holy Spirit that the gifts offered by human hands be consecrated, that is, become Christ's Body and Blood." At Mass "*the Church—and in particular the Church here and now gathered—offers* in the Holy Spirit the spotless Victim to the Father" (*General Instruction on the Roman Missal*, no. 79).

This is what we really go to Mass for: not only to praise and thank God, important as that is, not only to hear God speaking to us personally in the reading of his words, essential as that also is. The key to it all, the "church's intention" in summoning us to celebrate together, is to offer Christ as "priests in the Priest," and to offer ourselves—through him, with him, and in him—as "victims in the Victim."

So here is what you need to do. When the presider lifts up the host the first time, after quoting Jesus' words, "This is my body, given for you," you need to repeat those words in your heart. You need to say them with Jesus and as Jesus, whose body you became at baptism, speaking as his body on earth, making these words—as they were for Jesus—the most important words of your life: "This is my body, given for you."

Given to whom? Given to God but also to every member of the human race. To your family, to the people kneeling next to you, you are saying, "This is my body, given for you." To all the people in the church you are saying, "This is my body, given for you." To every member of the human race—to the most saintly and most sinful, to the drug addicts, rapists, and suicide bombers, to everyone for whom Jesus offered himself on the cross—you are saying, "This is my body, given for you."

And how are you given? How, in practice, do you give your "flesh for the life of the world"? It is very simple. In every encounter with another person, in everything you say and do, you surrender your body to Jesus as a "living sacrifice," to let Jesus express himself to others in and through your human, physical words and gestures. You let Jesus communicate life to others by giving expression to his life in you. You express your faith—his divine truth invisible within you—in visible, human words. You let him express his invisible, divine love in you through your audible, human actions. In this way you give "your flesh for the life of the world" by letting the invisible life of God in you "take flesh" in physical, visible expression to others. All day, every day. To every person you meet.

Concretely, you could begin, as suggested above, with a very specific nut that just might fit your bolt: Form the habit of telling everyone you meet whatever you see in them that is good. This is a concrete way to say in action to every person you deal with: "This is my body, given for you."

This is why God the Son became flesh: to give his body to us and for us. This is what we did at baptism: we entered into the mystery of his death and resurrection by "presenting our bodies as a living sacrifice" to be incorporated into Jesus' body on the cross so that we might offer ourselves and be offered in the act of dying with him and in him as members of the body hanging on the cross.

That is the mystery of the Mass. It is the only way we can participate "fully, actively, and consciously" in Eucharist as the bishops at the Second Vatican Council said we must be led to do:

> *It is very much the wish of the Church that all the faithful should be led to take that full, conscious, and active part in liturgical celebrations which is demanded by the very nature of the liturgy, and to which the Christian people, "a chosen race, a royal priesthood, a redeemed people" have a right and to which they are bound by reason of their baptism. (On the Sacred Liturgy, no. 14)*

Communion: A Preview of Heaven

Suppose everyone were actually given to everyone else. Suppose everyone on earth let Jesus as "Christ," Prophet, Priest, and King express himself—his truth, his love, his response to every situation—in and through their every word and action. This world would be a paradise—the kingdom of God would be realized.

It would not yet be "heaven on earth." For that we have to be freed from the restrictions of our physical way of knowing things and brought into the face-to-face encounter of perfect union with God.

It is true that "we are God's children now." We have "become Christ" the Son. But Christ has not yet grown "to full stature" in us.

We still have thoughts, desires, and actions that are not completely conformed to his. While we are sometimes only too painfully aware of what we are not, it is essential to bear in mind that "what we will be has not yet been revealed." John assures us: "What we do know is this: when God is perfectly revealed, we will be like him, for we will see him as he is" (1 John 3:2). The moment in the Mass that gives us a preview of this is the Rite of Communion.

The Rite of Communion begins with the petitions of the Our Father, all of which are asking for the realization of the "end time"— when Christ returns in triumph at the end of the world, and the priorities of his own heart, what he came to accomplish on earth, will be realized.

- *The Father will be perfectly known and loved by all of his children: "Hallowed be thy Name!"*

- *The "reign of God" will be established in every heart, and over every area and activity of human life in heaven and on earth: "Thy kingdom come!"*

- *Every heart, every human action, choice, and desire, will be totally surrendered to the will of the Father: "Thy will be done on earth as it is in heaven."*

- *When our surrender is complete, we will only be asking for one thing: "Give us today our daily bread, and forgive us our sins as we forgive those who sin against us."*[13]

These last seem to be two petitions, but in reality they are only one. The "daily bread" we ask for is Christ himself: Jesus the Bread of the heavenly banquet; Jesus the joy of the "wedding feast of the Lamb." And this Bread is only given in a communal meal. There is no private takeout. Only those who agree to sit down at table with the rest of the human race, with all of the redeemed without exception, in total mutual forgiveness and acceptance, can "eat bread in the kingdom of God." If we do not all forgive one another as God forgives us, there can be no wedding banquet. So we ask for these together.

And we experience their reality—not perfectly, but in preview—in the Rite of Communion, which in the liturgy is introduced by the words, "Blessed are those who are called to the supper [the wedding banquet] of the Lamb."

When we receive Communion together, we are all at peace—at least for that moment. All conflicts and divisions are set aside. We have seen with our own eyes Jesus entering into the body—and so into the heart—of every person present. How can we not accept one another? How can we not appreciate those to whom we, with our own eyes, have seen Jesus physically giving himself?

When the presider elevated the Body of Christ before Communion, he proclaimed, "Behold the Lamb of God; behold him who takes away the sins of the world." The sins of all present have not just been forgiven; they have been taken away. Annihilated. In the time frame of God they ceased to exist on the day of our baptism, when we, with all the sins we ever had or ever would commit, were incorporated into the body of Christ on the cross, died in him, and came back to earth as a "new creation."

When we rose out of the waters of baptism, Jesus rose from the dead in us. We gave him our bodies as a "living sacrifice" to be his body, to let him continue his presence and mission on earth in us. This is what we live for. This is all we live for. And God sees us now as we will be at the "end time," when "the marriage of the Lamb has come, and his bride has made herself ready." And "ready" means perfect. Paul tells us God "chose us in Christ before the foundation of the world to be holy and blameless before him in love."

Christ loved the church and gave himself up for her, in order to make her holy by cleansing her with the washing of water by the word, so as to present her to himself in all her glory, without stain or wrinkle or any other blemish, but holy and blameless. (Ephesians 5:25–27)

In the Rite of Communion we see made visible "the glory of this mystery, which is Christ in you, the hope of glory."

At this moment of the Mass, if we pay attention, we realize that in the eyes of God—who sees all of time, past, present, and future, in one act, as one eternal "now"—we are perfect now. God loves us now as we will be then. And that is how we must love one another. The Rite of Communion is a preview of this.

After all have received the Body and Blood of Christ, the liturgy calls for a time of silence. No words, no singing. It is a time to get in touch with what we are experiencing, a time to "feel" the peace and unity present in that moment, a time to penetrate the veil and savor a foretaste of heaven.

After Communion, we are aware, with Julian of Norwich, that, in the end, "all shall be well...all manner of things shall be well." We are assured there is a happy ending. And all things are well now, because Christ has conquered. We "seek peace" and find it.

At the end of Mass we rest briefly as we will at the "end of the day." We remind ourselves—by entering into the experience of it—that we have reason to be at peace right now. We immerse ourselves in the "end time," when:

> The wolf shall live with the lamb, the leopard shall lie down with the kid, the calf and the lion together, and a little child shall lead them…They will not hurt or destroy on all my holy mountain; for the earth will be full of the knowledge of the LORD as the waters cover the sea (Isaiah 11:6–9).

This preview of victory, this foretaste of the "peace and unity of the kingdom," gives us peace; but it also inspires us—it encourages us and motivates us to go out and work to make it happen.

At baptism we were consecrated stewards of his kingship. As the celebration of Eucharist ends, God gives us a glimpse of what it will be like when "the mystery of his will" is accomplished: God's "plan for the fullness of time, to gather up all things in him, things in heaven and things on earth."

We who see the world now divided and at war—the members of the Lord's own flock "harassed and helpless, scattered like sheep without a shepherd"—must bring to this picture the perspective of the end time. The Rite of Communion calls us to see Christ already reigning as King, "seated at the right hand of the Father." We look forward to the "blessed hope" of his second coming (adventum) and the "manifestation (epiphaniam) of the glory of our great God and Savior, Jesus Christ."[14]

Persevering in this hope, laboring to bring about the reign of God on earth though we feel at times nothing but helplessness and hopelessness, is a mystical experience. During the Rite of Communion embrace that experience, and because of it, renew your determination to shoulder your responsibility as a "steward of the kingship of Christ" and exercise leadership in bringing about changes on earth.

Getting down to the nuts and bolts of this, just renew your resolve to notice anything around you that calls for change. God will take you the rest of the way!

CONCLUSION
Your Choice

We were created to "know, love, and serve God." And all the baptized are called to do this perfectly: to grow to that fullness of life that is the perfection of love. That is our goal—to know and love God "in Christ" as deeply and passionately as God knows and loves us. God calls us to do great things, and God empowers us to do them as the body of Jesus acting on earth today with us, in us, and through us!

These simple nuts and bolts are an easy, practical, and profitable way to get started.

All you have to do is begin.

NOTES

1. In addition to *The Jerome Biblical Commentary,* all I can suggest here are a few names, solid and spiritual: Raymond Brown (multiple books, especially on the Gospels); John L. McKenzie (*Dictionary of the Bible,* and especially *The Two-Edged Sword* for the Old Testament, *The Power and the Wisdom* for the New Testament); Bruce Vawter (*A Path Through Genesis*). For a spiritually inspired and surprising explanation of the church's moral teaching, read Bernard Häring (e.g., *Priesthood Imperiled*). Also important are books by women, for example, Barbara Reid (*Choosing the Better Part?: Women in the Gospel of Luke*) and Elizabeth Johnson (*Truly Our Sister*).

2. This makes us ask what image of the church we are working out of. Do we see the church, and ourselves, as a community designed by God to be in the image of the Trinity, where Father, Son and Spirit find their identity and distinction as Persons through the relationship they have with one another?

The "distinction of roles" in the Trinity does not destroy their unity, because they are "equal in majesty, undivided in splendor." What does this say about any "distinction of roles" in the church that is accompanied by the separating "splendor" of prestige and preferential protocol? By differences in dress and title that give the impression that those in some positions are "higher" and more important than others? Pope Francis is reacting against this by setting an example of simplicity that has delighted the world.

3. Encarta® World English Dictionary © 1999 Microsoft Corporation.

4. This explanation is drawn from Wikipedia, "Peak Experiences."

5. For an explanation of this and of how to do it, see his book *Choosing Life*, Paulist Press, 1978. This is, or should be, a spiritual classic.

6. Saint Paul uses the expression "in Christ" or its equivalent 164 times to express the mystery of our incorporation into Christ. This is the basic theme of his letters. See Fernand Prat, S.J., *The Theology of St. Paul*, tr. John Stoddard, Vol. II (Burns Oates & Washbourne, 1934).

Jesus said in Matthew 11:27: "No one knows the Father but the Son." This was not a simple statement of fact, as if it just so happened that no one had gotten to know the Father but himself. It was a statement of principle: no one is capable of knowing the Father but the Son. To know God as he is—to "know" the Father in the way Jesus is talking about—one must be God. This is what God is: God is the one whose nature it is to be able to know God as he is. No one, therefore, who is not God by nature can possibly know or be enabled to know God as he is in himself. God himself cannot make a creature able to know him as he is, because this would be a contradiction in terms. God's very essence, his very being and life, is to know and love himself as he actually is. This is what makes

God God. It is unique to him. It presupposes Infinite Being, for only the Infinite can know the Infinite as it is. Nothing finite that God can create could possibly have this power.

But Jesus claims that anyone can know the Father to whom "the Son wishes to reveal him."

This can only mean one thing: Since it is impossible for anyone to know God as he is except God—since "no one knows the Father but the Son"—the only way we can know God as God is to become God. The only way we can know the Father is to become the Son. We can know God as he is only by sharing in God's own nature—for to know God as he is, is something inseparable from the nature of God; it is indistinguishable from actually being God himself. To know the Father we must be the Son:

To really "reveal the Father" to us, Jesus must draw us into his very life, share his own divine nature with us, let us live and be "in him" as "sons in the Son." Then we can know the Father by participating in Jesus' own act of knowing, for it will not be we alone, but Jesus himself who is knowing the Father in us and catching us up in his own knowing act.

Can we believe in such an identification with Christ? Can we believe that in him we actually share in the life and nature of God himself? That is the mystery of "grace."

7. This mystery of "partnership" with Christ is another basic theme of St. Paul's letters. Twenty-nine times he uses the prefix syn- in Greek ("co-" in English) to express our union with Christ, as members of his body, in what he did and we do. Fernand Prat, S.J., gives the list in his *The Theology of St. Paul*, Vol. II, pages 18–20

and 391–395: co-suffer: Romans 8:17, 1 Corinthians 12:26; co-crucified: Romans 6:6, Galatians 2:20; co-die: 2 Timothy 2:11, cf. 2 Corinthians 7:3; co-buried: Romans 6:4, Colossians 2:12; co-resurrected: Ephesians 2:6, Colossians 2:12, 3:1; co-live: Romans 6:8; co-vivified (returned to life): Ephesians 2:5, Colossians 2:13; co-formed (configured): Philippians 3:10, Romans 8:21; co-glorified: Romans 8:17; co-seated: Ephesians 2:6; co-reign: 2 Timothy 2:12; cf. 1 Corinthians 4:8; co-planted: Romans 6:5; co-heirs: Romans 8:17, Ephesians 3:6; co-sharers: Ephesians 3:6, 5:7; co-incarnated (embodied): Ephesians 3:6; co-built: Ephesians 2:22; co-structured (and connected): Ephesians 2:21, Ephesians 4:16, Colossians 2:19. And add 1 Corinthians 3:9: co-workers with God (synergoi), quoted in Vatican II on "Missionary Activity," no. 15, and 2 Corinthians 6:1: co-working (synergountes).

8. General Instruction on the Roman Missal, 2002, nos. 29, 55–56.

9. Sure, God can just put thoughts into our heads "out of the blue" if he wants. We call those "special inspirations," and they don't depend on anything we do—"The wind blows where it chooses." But normally God gives grace—lets us share in his divine life—in and through our human actions.

10. General Instruction on the Roman Missal, 2002, nos. 29, 55–56.

11. You will find Jesus' "New Law" explained in my book *Make Me a Sabbath of Your Heart*, Dimension Books; republished by His Way Communications, www.hisway.com.

12. The Cursillos de Cristiandad ("short courses in Christianity") began in the 1940s after the Civil War in Spain when a Catholic Action group met to try to put their country together again. The first Cursillo in the United States was held in Waco, Texas, in 1957. The movement spread throughout the country and the world. Today it is a worldwide movement with centers in Australia, Austria, Canada, France, Germany, Great Britain, Ireland, Italy, Japan, Korea, Mexico, New Zealand, Philippines, Puerto Rico, Portugal, Sri Lanka, Taiwan, United States, Yugoslavia, and several African countries.

The purpose of the Cursillo Movement is to bring about change in the environments where Christians live. Those who have gone through the 3-day "weekend" and are living the Cursillo method become agents for change in their families, work situations, neighborhoods, social gatherings, and culture. Cursillistas are a part of the Christian community that links together with others to bring Jesus Christ to the world.

13. This is the official translation authorized by the bishops of New Zealand.

14. The new English translation of the Mass substitutes St. Jerome's Latin Vulgate translation of Titus 2:13—adventum: "coming"— for epiphaniam, "manifestation," which is a more authentic reading. But both concepts are good and helpful.

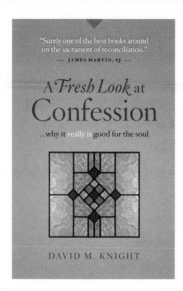